Robert Lowe was a full-time law lecturer for over twenty years. Since 1980 he has combined a divorce and litigation practice wit[illegible]
of [illegible]

Also in Hamlyn Paperbacks

QUESTIONS OF LAW by Bill Thomas
QUESTIONS OF MOTORING LAW by John Spencer
QUESTIONS OF LAW: HOMES by Trevor M. Aldridge

QUESTIONS OF DIVORCE LAW

Robert Lowe

Hamlyn Paperbacks

QUESTIONS OF DIVORCE LAW

ISBN 0 600 20427 8

First published in Great Britain 1983
by Hamlyn Paperbacks

Hamlyn Paperbacks are published by
The Hamlyn Publishing Group Ltd,
Astronaut House, Feltham,
Middlesex, England

Made and printed in Great Britain by
Hazell Watson & Viney Ltd
Aylesbury, Bucks

Introduction

In this book I have tried to give practical information and advice to people with marital problems for whom divorce is one possible option. These last words are important because, in the words of the Law Commission for England and Wales, a good divorce law should seek to achieve two objects:

1 to buttress, rather than to undermine the stability of marriage, and

2 when regrettably a marriage has irretrievably broken down, to enable the empty legal shell to be destroyed with the maximum fairness and the minimum of bitterness, distress and humiliation.

Logically the first question (not always apparent to a husband or wife struggling with a difficult marriage) is to ask whether a marriage can be saved. So the first part of Chapter 1 is devoted to this topic. I also mention the growing topic of conciliation which can help to take the heat out of the situation and enable the parties to make sensible and rational decisions of lasting benefit to themselves and, above all, to their children. A list of useful addresses is set out at the back of this book.

In the vast majority of cases the task of getting a divorce is very simple but the breakdown of a marriage usually involves a host of difficult problems—child welfare, money, housing, tax, social security and personal protection. Few couples can cope with such problems unassisted—especially at a time of great emotional and financial stress. Many people are reluctant to go to a lawyer because of the fear of the likely cost. In Chapter 2 I have tried to banish some of these fears by explaining what a case is likely to cost and how legal aid and 'Green Form' assistance can help persons of modest means. In the remaining five chapters I examine some of many problems which have to be faced once a decision has been taken to end the marriage.

Divorce law does not stand still, and it is quite likely that there will be important changes before long. Legal aid may become available for parents in care cases. The present 'three-year rule' for divorce (see page 58) may be replaced by a new rule forbidding any divorce in the first year of a marriage. The split between the High Court and the county courts may be changed so that all the most difficult cases go to the High Court. A change in the law may make it possible for an English court to award maintenance even where the divorce was obtained abroad. Finally, and most important, there may be an alteration in the maintenance law to bring it into line with divorce law which allows the parties to make a fresh start if their marriage has irretrievably broken down. Under a new law

1 the court would have to give overriding priority to the needs of the children;

2 conduct would become more relevant;

3 the courts could order a clean break; and

4 the courts would regard maintenance for a former wife as a short-term provision to enable her to adjust to her new situation after a divorce.

This book covers the law as it stands on 11th February 1983.

Robert Lowe

1 The Marriage Breaking Down

COUNSELLING

I just can't stand it any more, but I'm not sure if I want a divorce. Should I try marriage guidance? Would it stop me getting a divorce if it didn't work?

Let me answer the second question first: the answer is No. You can get a divorce if your marriage has irretrievably broken down, and the fact that you have been to marriage guidance will not cut down your rights in any way.

The object of seeing a marriage guidance counsellor (either alone or with your spouse) is to explore your feelings and attitudes and to see whether some adjustment on either side can bring about any improvement in your marriage. After all, marriage can be a very difficult relationship, and perhaps too many people rush into divorce as the easy option at the first sign of trouble. A visit to a marriage guidance counsellor can be a painful experience because the counsellor (and you) will search for the underlying causes of the problem, and you may have to recognise that, beneath the surface, much of the trouble stems from your own inadequacies or from your lack of understanding of your partner. The success or failure of counselling will depend to a large degree on whether you and/or your partner are prepared to face up to the situation in its true light and then to work at improving it. If, at the end of the day, you or your partner decide that things can't improve, then divorce may well be the only solution.

Do many people use marriage guidance?

Let me give you some figures which have been produced by the National Marriage Guidance Council. In 1981, a year in which divorce topped the 150,000 mark, the 160 Marriage Guidance Councils which make up the National Marriage Guidance Council handled 36,000 cases and conducted a total of 202,000 interviews. Interviews with wives (84,000) outnumbered interviews with husbands (37,000) by more than two to one, and in addition there were 66,000 interviews where the husband and wife came together. This last figure shows the most dramatic increase over the last eleven years: the total number of interviews went up from 87,500 in 1970 to 202,000 in 1980, while the number of joint interviews soared from 6,000 to 66,000.

My husband thinks that marriage guidance is a lot of rubbish, and he certainly won't go there. Is there any point in my going there alone?

Certainly. You can see from the figures given in the previous answer that very many interviews take place with only one of the couple. The interview may help you to understand more clearly why your marriage is in trouble and may give you some ideas for improving it.

I've talked to my friends and to my family about my marriage problems, and I don't see how I can get any more help by going to see a counsellor.

There are two things to say here. First of all, your friends and your family are very close to your wife and yourself, and it is not easy for them to talk to you in an unemotional sensible way. There is a lot to be gained by explaining your problems to someone who is a complete stranger to both of you. He or she will listen to you and will form an objective professional view as to where the problem lies.

Secondly, you must bear in mind that a counsellor has had special training for dealing with marital problems—something which your family and friends, however well intentioned, have not had.

It's all so embarrassing that I can't bear to talk about it – especially to a complete stranger.

Counsellors have been specially trained to listen sympathetically to all their clients and to do so in a way which will cut down the embarrassment to a minimum. Try it – you will see that I am right.

He has said that he will kill me if he finds out that I have been to marriage guidance. If I do go along, can I be absolutely sure that he won't find out?

Yes. The marriage guidance service treats every interview (including the name of the client) as entirely confidential.

I know that I have done some terrible things and if I go to marriage guidance I'm sure they won't understand and will blame me for having destroyed our marriage.

That's where you are wrong. Marriage guidance counsellors will *never* blame you for what you may have done—it is not their job to sit in judgement on the client. They are there essentially to listen and then to talk to you to see if there are any ways of improving your marriage.

The sexual part of our marriage has always been bad, and that's the cause of all the problems. How can a counsellor possibly help in a case like that?

There are three things to say about that. First of all, it is very unlikely that sex has been the only problem. Secondly, all counsellors receive sex therapy training, so that they are likely to have something helpful to say. Thirdly, the counsellor may be able to refer you to a sex clinic where you will be seen by a specialist in sexual problems.

What can counsellors do to improve a marriage?

Many clients feel that they just want to be able to talk, and they feel a tremendous sense of relief and release when they can talk to someone who knows how to listen. This of itself can be a first step towards a possible improvement in the marriage.

Is there any point in going to a counsellor if we've already decided to separate?

Yes. If you go on your own, you may still achieve what counsellors' call 'personal growth', which would help you not only in your continuing relationship with your spouse, but also in your other relationships. If you both decide that you need help to sort everything out, then that is the point where counselling stops and conciliation begins (see below).

If I go to a counsellor, will I have to pay anything?

Some counsellors charge a modest sum (perhaps £9 per hour) for their services, but others don't. You certainly won't be asked to pay anything if you are receiving supplementary benefit or family income supplement.

CONCILIATION

You referred to something called 'conciliation'. Isn't that the same thing as counselling?

No, it is not. Counselling, as I have said, is concerned with attitudes and emotions and is not aimed at solving a specific legal problem. Conciliation, on the other hand, is concerned with a particular issue (perhaps the custody of a child) in a case where legal proceedings are taking place or are imminent.

The conciliators encourage the husband and wife to reach an agreement as an alternative to an unpleasant fight in the courts. In other words, conciliation can help to take the heat out of an explosive situation by making the parties see that an agreed solution is in the interests of both of them (and of their children), in both the short and the long term.

A pilot scheme was established in Bristol in 1979 and the early indications are encouraging. Conciliators, solicitors and clients work closely together, and good results can be achieved if:

1 the conciliator is brought in early enough, before attitudes have hardened, and

2 he or she can persuade the parties that the sole aim is to bring about an agreed decision and *not* to force a solution on them.

Will the conciliation service expand?

Well, there is at present some doubt about the Bristol Scheme and whether it will receive a grant which will enable it to carry on. There has however been an interesting development in the High Court in London. As from 1st January 1983 they have started a conciliation service in cases where there is a dispute about the custody of or access to the children. It is hoped that an informal hearing before the registrar (a court official) and private talks with a court welfare officer will help the couple to reach agreement and to avoid the bitterness and recrimination which a fight over the children usually causes.

JUDICIAL SEPARATION

My friends have said that we ought to have a legal separation. What does that mean?

It can mean one of two things. First of all, you may decide to live apart by agreement and make your own arrangements as to such things as money and who is to have the children. Secondly, it may be possible to get a decree of judicial separation from a county court or an order from a magistrates' court.

What is a judicial separation?

Basically it is a decree stating that a married couple are no longer bound to live together. You can get a decree if you can prove one of five grounds. These grounds are the same as the 'facts' for divorce (see page 57), and there is no need to show that your marriage has broken down irretrievably. If you want a decree as soon as you split up there are only two grounds, namely:

1 that your spouse has committed adultery and you find it intolerable to live with him or her, or

2 that your spouse has behaved in such a way that you cannot reasonably be expected to live with him or her.

As to the effect of a decree of judicial separation, I have already mentioned the main point: you are still married, but you are no longer bound to live together. There is also a very old rule that a husband cannot be guilty of raping his wife because she is treated as consenting to sexual intercourse (although, strangely enough, the husband *can* be convicted of assault if he uses force). This so-called consent to intercourse comes to an end on judicial separation, so that a conviction for rape is possible. Finally, the change in your relationship is reflected in the rules governing inheritance if you die without leaving a will. Normally your husband or wife will inherit a very large part (and often the whole) of your estate, but if a decree of judicial separation is in force at the date of death, the spouse will not inherit anything.

Apart from the above matters a decree of judicial separation is useful as evidence that you are living apart. You may, for example, want to prove this to a housing department or to the Inspector of Taxes.

If I get a judicial separation, can I get a divorce afterwards?

Yes, you can, and the decree can be useful to prove the relevant facts. If, for example, the decree was granted on the 'adultery and intolerability' ground, the divorce registrar may accept the previous decree as sufficient evidence of the adultery (so that you would not have to prove the adultery all over again when you applied for a divorce).

In practice, the number of petitions for judicial separation decrees are minute when compared to divorce petitions (in 1977 the figures were 1,980 and 167,074 respectively) and they are usually sought by

1 persons who have religious objections to divorce, or

2 persons who still hope that their marriage can be saved, or

3 persons who have not been married for three years (see page 58).

One final point: the powers of the court to make financial orders are exactly the same as on a divorce.

SEPARATION BY AGREEMENT

You said something about living apart by agreement. Does the agreement have to be in writing, and does it have to be signed?

The answer to both questions is No. In practice, there is a lot to be said for having a written agreement drawn up because (for example) it will greatly reduce arguments as to what was agreed. Also, under the Income Tax Acts a husband and wife will be taxed separately if they are living apart. One way of proving this is to show that they are separated by agreement, and a written agreement will clearly be very useful for this purpose.

My husband says that he wants to settle his finances once and for all. He is offering to let me have the house and £10,000 if I promise not to make any further claims against him or his estate. What happens if I agree? Can I get more money if I find that I just can't pay the bills?

In law an agreement not to claim any further sums is not legally binding. If, therefore, you find that you cannot pay the bills, you can ask him for some money and, if he doesn't pay, you could take him to court on the ground that he has failed to provide reasonable maintenance. Alternatively, the court has power to rewrite the agreement. If there is a divorce the court can grant you financial provision despite your agreement not to claim it.

That is the theory; whether you will succeed is another matter. If, for example, the agreement has been in force for a long time, and if both of you had good legal advice when you made it, the agreement may well be upheld.

One further point: if there is a divorce the court can sometimes make a 'clean break' order which will stop you coming back for more money (see page 88).

TAX AND SOCIAL SECURITY

Will separation reduce our tax bill?

There will usually be a tax saving in the year of separation because the wife's income for that year is split into two parts. For her earned income up to the time of separation she will get the usual wife's earned income allowance. In addition (and this is where the saving comes in) she will get a full single person's allowance for all her income (earned and unearned) arising after separation *and*, if she has children living with her, she will also get the so-called 'single parent' allowance. For a wife who has an income of her own the timing of the separation can be important (although a battered wife is unlikely to be influenced by tax considerations). The husband will get the married man's personal allowance in the usual way. You should tell the tax office straight away when the separation takes place, and they will then make any necessary adjustments to your PAYE coding.

What about the years after the separation?

You are taxed in the same way as two unmarried persons, and a working couple with children will usually pay less tax than before separation. Also, if the husband makes maintenance payments to his wife under an order or agreement, then a tax saving is possible (see page 115). In general the income tax position of a separated couple is similar to that of a couple who are divorced.

I am receiving supplementary benefit for myself and for my six-year-old daughter. Can I get more money by taking my husband to court?

You can certainly take your husband to the county court or magistrates' court on the grounds of his desertion or behaviour or because he has failed to provide reasonable maintenance, but this is unlikely to improve your overall cash position. Even if the court makes an order in favour of yourself and/or your daughter, you will only get 'more money' if the maintenance comes to more than the benefit which you are getting (and sometimes not even then).

Benefit is only payable in so far as your 'resources' fall short of your 'requirements'. Maintenance is a 'resource' which will reduce the amount of benefit to which you are entitled. If, therefore, you are receiving weekly benefit of £35, this will be cut down by the amount of maintenance awarded.

One final point: even if the maintenance comes to more than the benefit, you could still be no better off and you might well be worse off. If you are claiming supplementary benefit, you will also be entitled to certain other benefits such as free school meals and free medical prescriptions. If the maintenance takes you over the supplementary benefit limits, then these other benefits will also be lost.

Do these rules about maintenance also apply if I am drawing family income supplement?

Yes, they do.

What happens if I do get an order, and he then stops paying?

At one time many wives suffered great hardship in this

situation because their secure income from supplementary benefit was replaced by the worry and uncertainty of a maintenance order which might or might not be paid. Fortunately, there is now a way of avoiding this hardship. You can 'sign over' your rights under the order to the DHSS. You can then collect benefit in the usual way, and the clerk of the court will send the maintenance to the DHSS. They will probably ask you to sign a form giving the court power to chase up your husband if he defaults.

My wife is being looked after by the DHSS. Why should I pay her any money?

Supplementary benefit is in the nature of a 'safety net', and Parliament has said very clearly that a husband must support his wife and children if he is able to do so. Conversely, it is the duty of a wife to support her husband and children if she is able to do so.

Even if your wife does not take you to court, the DHSS can do so, and the court can order you to reimburse the DHSS in whole or in part for the sums which they have paid to your wife. You could also find yourself criminally liable for not supporting them when you were in a position to do so.

If, of course, your own income isn't very high, you may be able to persuade the court not to make a maintenance order which would reduce your own income below subsistence level.

MAGISTRATES' COURTS

I don't want to leave my husband, but he is very irresponsible about money and never gives me enough. Can I take him to court?

Yes. If you can prove that he has failed to provide you with reasonable maintenance, an order can be made against him by a magistrates' court even though you are living together.

Such an order can be enforced in the usual way (perhaps by deduction from his earnings) for six months. Unfortunately such an order is likely to lead to an early separation!

Recently I lost my job and am unemployed. I live with a woman who has a good job. My wife is now taking me to the magistrates' court because I have deserted her and is asking for maintenance for herself and the children. Must I pay?

I don't think so. The court has to do what it can on the basis of *your* income and not the income of the woman with whom you are living. Since you have no income (apart from unemployment benefit) the court will not make a maintenance order against you. They may, however, make a nominal order of perhaps 5p per year. This will give your wife the right to come back to get the amount increased if you do get a job at some future time.

Since my husband left me for another woman six months ago I have been struggling to make ends meet. I am in danger of getting my electricty cut off and I owe money to a store who supplied me with clothing for my children. Can I get my husband to pay these bills?

Yes. You can ask him to pay the bills and, if he doesn't pay, you can take out a summons in the local magistrates' court on the ground of his desertion or on the ground of his failure to provide reasonable maintenance. If you prove your case, the magistrates can order him to pay not only maintenance, but also lump sums of up to £500 for yourself and for each child of the family, and this should help you pay the bills.

What happens if he can't pay over the money all at once?

The court can order him to make payments by instalments.

You could also consider this type of order if, for example, you are struggling to meet monthly hire purchase payments. It will be extremely handy if your husband's money comes in just as the HP collector is due to call.

A friend has offered to lend me the money. Does that affect my right to claim it from my husband?

No. The magistrates can order your husband to pay you a lump sum to cover any liability incurred by you (in this case the loan) for the maintenance of yourself and the children. So you can borrow the money from your friend and then claim a lump sum from your husband. You can then use that lump sum to repay the loan. But be careful: there is no guarantee that the court would make such an order.

My wife is taking me to the magistrates' court. She is asking for custody of the children. I can't look after them myself, but I want to have a say in their upbringing. What do I do?

You should explain the position to the magistrates and ask them to make what I might call a 'shared rights' order. This is an order which gives your wife legal custody, but which allows you to keep some of the rights and duties relating to your children and to exercise them jointly with your wife. The court will decide which rights and duties you can share, and they will be listed in the order.

My husband and I have split up after a disastrous marriage, but neither of us wants a divorce. He has agreed to pay me £30 per week and also a sum of £1000 so that I can decorate the flat. Can I go to court to have this agreement written into a court order?

Yes. A magistrates' court can make an order for payment of agreed periodic amounts and an agreed lump sum—and there is no £500 ceiling in this case. The court is not bound to make an order, and it must be satisfied that it is in the interests of justice to do so.

What does that mean?

This is a fairly new rule, and there have been no decided cases on it. If, for example, a wife was receiving supplementary benefit, and if a husband agreed to pay far less than he could afford to pay, then an order might well be refused. The court might feel that the husband was, in effect, passing over to the state his own maintenance obligations which he could well afford to pay.

What is the advantage of getting a court order in this sort of case?

There are three advantages. Firstly, an order gives you greater protection if your husband should default – it is easier to enforce. Secondly, there are tax advantages. Payments to a spouse under a court order not exceeding £33 per week or £143 per month are known as 'small maintenance payments', and they are paid gross; this can obviously be helpful if cash is tight. If, however, the payments are made under an agreement, then this rule does not apply, and the payer must deduct tax when he makes the payments. If the order relates to children, it may be possible to reduce the tax bill on the basis that the maintenance payments are income of the child (see page 116). Finally an order (but not an agreement) can be signed over to the DHSS (see page 18).

OCCUPATION OF HOME

My husband has left me. Can I go on living in the house?

As a wife you have a right to live in the home; this means that your husband cannot turn you out without a court order. If the house is rented, you will probably have the protection of the Rent Acts; this will mean that your landlord cannot turn you out without a court order, and this can only be made on certain grounds (such as non-payment of rent). You will have this protection even in cases where your husband is the tenant. You can also take steps to stop your husband selling the house over your head. I will explain this more fully in Chapter 4 (see page 102).

My husband has left me in our flat and has gone to live with his girlfriend. Can he turn me out by just going along to the landlord and giving up his rent-book?

No. Under the Rent Acts you are protected in this sort of case. You must, however, make sure that you don't give the landlord any ground for possession, and so the first thing to do is to find out what is happening about the rent. This is a very difficult area of the law, and you should seek legal advice straightaway.

I have just had a letter from my landlords saying that they have got a possession order against my husband for not paying his rent and that I've got to leave within four weeks. What should I do?

Before the order was made you had a right to occupy the house, and you could have kept the landlord at bay by paying the rent (with the help of housing benefit from the local housing authority). In this case it may be possible for you to appeal against the order, and the court may then allow you to stay if they are satisfied that the rent will be paid.

My husband and I are still living in the same house, but it's becoming unbearable. I don't want to turn him out but I do want to have a few hours to myself in the evenings. Can the courts deal with this sort of problem.

Yes: if you really want to go to court, then you can do so. Under an Act called the Matrimonial Homes Act 1967 the court can do many things, and one of them is to 'regulate' the rights of occupation of both of you. They can, for example, say that your husband shall not come into the living room between the hours of 8 and 10 pm from Monday to Friday. It can also work the other way round: if your husband works from home the court can also say that you must not go into the room which he uses as his office. However, I feel it is ridiculous to go to court over this sort of problem and I suggest you sort it out by agreement.

My wife is very nasty to me and keeps on telling me to leave. She says that if I don't go soon she will tell her solicitor to start court proceedings to have me thrown out. Naturally I don't want to leave. Should I do so? Can I be ordered out?

The answer to your first question is No. If you genuinely feel that your marriage is going through a bad spell which will pass, then you should certainly stay and do what you can to improve the relationship. A husband often puts himself in a weak position if he just leaves at the first sign of trouble.

If, however, you feel that the marriage is finished, then you should have a long talk with your wife about ending it in a civilized manner. You should discuss money, the children and the future of the home, both short-term and long-term. In appropriate cases your solicitors can draw up an agreement. Perhaps you might agree to move out as one of the terms of that agreement.

Turning now to your second question, the answer is Yes, the court can turn you out under the Domestic Violence and Matrimonial Proceedings Act 1976 (the name is misleading). The court can order a husband or wife to leave the home *even though there is no violence at all.* In one case the judge said this:

'The court should think essentially of homes, especially for the children, and then consider the balance of hardship, being careful not to underestimate the difficulties which even single men have these days in finding somewhere to live.'

Does that really mean that a court will turn me out of my home merely for the sake of the children? I've done nothing wrong, and I think that's terrible.

There have been cases where the house has been a big one in which the husband and the wife could lead more or less separate lives. In these cases the courts have not taken the drastic step of ordering the husband or the wife out. In many cases, however, this will not be possible, and the courts can then make orders which many husbands regard as grossly unfair. Take, for example, the case of Mr and Ms Spindlow (they happened to be an unmarried couple, but that didn't affect the case).

Ms Spindlow left the flat with the children and went to stay with friends in overcrowded conditions. There was no violence, but there was a lot of tension, and this was harmful to the children. She asked for an order that Mr Spindlow should leave, and she got it. One of the judges said this:

'Somebody has got to provide a home for these small children. Clearly the person who can do it is Ms Spindlow. If it is clear . . . that she is not prepared to go back and share her home with Mr Spindlow, there is only one solution, namely that she must go back to the home, and he must leave . . . it is no good taking up a great deal of time talking in terms of blame or conduct. What we have to deal with is the reality of the situation which is that two children are in need of a home and are without one."

I should perhaps add that not all courts will look at a case in this way. There have been some judges who have asked a somewhat different question, namely, 'Did this wife behave reasonably in not going back to live with her husband?' This is obviously an area where you need legal advice so that your case can be presented to the court in the best possible way.

Will this mean that I will never be able to go back?

No. These exclusion orders are only intended to run for a short time, and the courts have said that they should not last for more than three months (though they can be renewed for a further period). They are in the nature of a stop-gap, and hopefully it will be possible for some more permanent arrangements to be made while the order is in force.

PERSONAL PROTECTION ORDER

I'm terrified of my husband and I want him out of the house. My friends tell me that this takes a long time. Is that right?

No. If your case is strong enough, you can get an order very quickly indeed from either a county court or from a magistrates' court—although the powers of the county court are somewhat wider. If you want an order restraining your husband from violence, this can be obtained within a matter of hours without any notice being given to him. On the other hand, an order to turn him out of the house may take a little longer. The papers must be sent or delivered to your husband (so that he can come to court and say why he should not be turned out of the house), and the hearing will not take place until a few days after this has been done.

The court has ordered my husband out of the home, but he keeps coming back. Can he be arrested and sent to prison?

A power of arrest can only be included in an exclusion order if the expelled spouse has injured the other spouse (or children) and is likely to do so again. If such a provision is included, then the police *may* arrest your husband and bring him before the court within 24 hours, if he is in breach of the order. Even if there is no power of arrest you can apply to have your husband committed to prison for contempt of court, and a magistrates' court can issue a warrant for his arrest.

In your last few answers you have said that the court can turn a husband out. Can the court also turn the wife out?

Yes, the powers of the court are exactly the same over the wife. But in general the court will allow the wife to stay in the house if she is the person who is looking after the children and providing a home for them.

My wife writes long letters to my managing director and telephones the members of my staff telling them about our sex life. She is making my life intolerable. Can I do anything about it?

Yes. Your wife is clearly guilty of molesting you, and the county court can make an order forbidding her from doing so. She will then be in contempt of court if she does it again.

I have left the house because I can't take any more violence. My baby is due in six months time. How can I get somewhere to live?

There are two things that you can do. The first, which I have already explained (see page 25), is to go to the county court or to a magistrates' court for an order that your husband should leave the house and that you should be allowed to move back in. As I have said, however, these orders are intended to last for only about three months. Secondly, you could ask your local authority to rehouse you under the Housing (Homeless Persons) Act 1977. Under this Act they are bound to rehouse you if:

1 you are homeless and
2 you did not become homeless intentionally and
3 you have a priority need, a term that includes pregnancy.

Are you technically homeless? I think you are. Your case is covered by a clause in the Act which says that a person is homeless even though he or she has some accommodation available if it is likely that there will be violence if he or she goes to live there. The second condition should create no problems for you; no one is going to say that a pregnant woman who leaves home because of violence has become homeless intentionally. So, then, the local authority are under a duty to rehouse you. Whether they will actually be able to give you anything other than overnight accommodation at a hostel is another matter.

My husband has turned me out and has changed the locks. My parents have a large house and have offered to put me up, but I don't really want to go back to them. Can I get a council flat?

You will probably find that there is a long waiting list for council accommodation, and so your only chance of getting immediate help is to show that you are 'homeless' under the Housing (Homeless Persons) Act 1977 (see above). The Act is very unpopular with local authorities, and many of them (especially in the inner cities) just do not have the necessary accommodation to carry out their statutory duties. I am rather afraid that the housing authority will decide that you are not homeless because accommodation in your parents' house is available to you.

SALE OF HOUSE

When we got married we bought a house in our joint names. We have now split up. Will the house have to be sold?

No. Either you or your spouse can ask the court to order a sale, but the court is not bound to do so. The court will do everything possible to preserve the house as a home; it may, for example, order one of you to buy out the other. The court will also want to know if a divorce case is going to be brought fairly soon. We shall see in Chapter 4 that the divorce court can deal with the house in many different ways, and so, if a divorce is imminent, the court is unlikely to order a sale before then.

We bought our house in our joint names, but my wife has moved out, and we are going to sell it. I've been paying the mortgage from the very beginning. Can I claim a larger slice of the sale money?

Basically the answer is No: the payments were merely one of your contributions to the marriage, and no doubt your wife contributed in other ways. The position is different, however, once your wife leaves. By making the mortgage repayments you are building up the value of one of your wife's assets (her half share in the house) and you may well be entitled to a 'credit' for one half of the capital repayments made by you since your wife left. Let us suppose, for example, that the proceeds of sale (after paying expenses and the mortgage) come to £20,500 and that you have repaid capital of £1,000 since your wife left. In this case you may be entitled to reclaim £500 of the proceeds of sale. This will leave £20,000 to be divided equally between you. The court will also want to know why your wife left; if your conduct drove her out, then the courts will not be so keen to apply the rules which I have described.

I am thinking of having an extension built on to our house, but our marriage isn't going too well and could crack up at any time. Will the extension be taken into account if we have to sell the house?

Yes. A husband or wife who makes a substantial improvement to the home (or indeed to any property) will find that this is reflected in the share to which he or she is entitled. The amount of your claim can be a matter for argument, but it will often be based on the improvement factor. Let us suppose that the house belongs to your wife; if 30 per cent of the increased value is due to the improvements, you should be able to claim 30 per cent of the net proceeds of the sale.

We are living in a house which is owned jointly by my wife and her mother. Do the same rules apply?

Yes, they do. Even if you don't own any part of the house before the improvements, you will end up as a part-owner of the property when the work has been carried out.

PAYMENT OF BILLS

My wife and I have split up, but I keep on getting bills from the department store where she has an account. These bills are getting bigger all the time. Can I just send them back unpaid?

There is one more thing which I need to know, and it is vital:

have you paid her bills in the past? If the answer is No, then you have no problems. You can return the bills unpaid with a note saying, 'These are my wife's debts, not mine.'

If on the other hand you have previously paid the store for goods supplied to your wife, then you must tell them straightaway that you will not pay her bills in future. You can then return unpaid any bills covering goods ordered by your wife *after* the store knew about the new arrangements. But I am afraid that you will still have to pay for goods ordered before that time. As a safety precaution the instructions should be confirmed in writing.

BANK ACOUNTS

We also have joint bank accounts into which I pay my salary. I don't want to find that she has spent it on herself. What do you advise?

I suggest that you open a new account for your salary. I also suggest that you draw out the bulk of your current salary while it is still there. You can notify her what you have done as soon as you have done it, and you can then discuss the whole question of financial support.

KIDNAPPED CHILDREN

While I was out shopping my husband just walked in and took the children. I am terrified that he is going to take them abroad. Can he be stopped?

The law can move very fast in these emergency cases. The first step is to make the child a ward of court – this can be done very quickly. Then a telephone call can be made to a department of the Home Office, and the person who takes the call can contact the various airports and seaports and tell them your husband's name (and the names of the children). With luck the officials who operate passport control will spot him or them and will not let them through. It might also be a good idea to telephone to the Passport Office in case your husband tries to get a new passport. It's vital to act very quickly in these cases, and I certainly can't guarantee that it will work. You should see a solicitor at once.

What happens if the courts are closed?

In that case your solicitor can go to see (or, in cases of extreme urgency, telephone) a judge at his home and get an order to stop your husband taking the children abroad. Your solicitor would have to promise that he will start court proceedings on the first available day, and he would have to make the necessary financial arrangements with you (either legal aid or private) to cover those proceedings. Once the judge has made the order (and some of them get rather cross if the telephone keeps ringing to disturb their TV viewing or their game of bridge!) your solicitor can contact the Passport Office and the Home Office in the way that I have described.

CHILDREN IN NEED OF CARE

I'm finding it very hard trying to bring up the children by myself. Can the local authority help?

Yes. You are obviously afraid that the children will be taken away from you, and I can well understand that. Under an Act called the Child Care Act 1980 the local authority must promote the welfare of children by cutting down the need to take children into care, or keeping them there, or bringing them before a juvenile court. The authority will offer you advice, guidance and assistance and, in exceptional circumstances, money. A social worker will talk to you about such things as payment of bills. He or she will also make sure that you are claiming all your legal rights – whether it is supplementary benefit, family income supplement, child benefit, one-parent benefit, housing benefit, free school meals, free prescriptions and so on. Taking a child into care is not only distressing for you, but it is also very expensive for the local authority, and everything will be done to avoid this.

Recently I've had a very worrying letter from the headmaster of my eldest boy's school, and I have also had visits from the health visitor and the police. Is there any danger that I might lose my children?

Yes, there is a danger. The local authority may take proceedings in the local juvenile court for what is known as a care order. These proceedings are known as care proceedings and are largely governed by an Act of Parliament called the Children and Young Persons Act 1969. The local authority must show one or more of several possible grounds. They include:

1 that the child is being avoidably neglected or is being ill-treated,
2 that the child is beyond parental control and
3 that the child has committed an offence.

They have also got to show that the child is in need of care or control which he or she is unlikely to receive unless the court makes an order.

Can I get legal aid for these care proceedings? I haven't got any money to pay for a solicitor.

You have no automatic right to legal aid. The rules are very complicated and unfair to parents. Basically the only parties before the court are the child (who can get legal aid) and the local authority. Normally the child will be represented by its parent, but the court can make an order that the parents shall not represent the child because their interests are different (that there is a 'conflict of interest' between them). Even here legal aid is not available to a parent, but this will soon be changed.

Incidentally, the legal aid in care proceedings is quite different from legal aid in matrimonial proceedings (which I shall describe in the next chapter). The main difference is that 'care' legal aid is granted (or not granted) by the court, while matrimonial legal aid is in the hands of committees appointed by the Law Society.

What happens if the local authority wins the case?

The court can do several things, but usually it will do one of two things. Firstly, it can make what is called a 'supervision order'. This means that the child will remain at home, but someone from the local authority or a probation officer will 'advise, assist and befriend' you. In other words, he will help you to cope. Secondly, the court can make a care order under which the child will be taken into care by the local authority who will then be responsible for his up-bringing until either the court discharges the order or the child attains the age of eighteen.

Can I appeal against a care order?

Yes, you can appeal to the Crown court.

GRANDPARENTAL ACCESS

My husband's mother was largely responsible for the break-up of our marriage, and we have furious rows because I won't let her see the children. She is threatening to take us to court so that she can get an access order. Can she do that?

No. There are some special rules dealing with access by grandparents, but they are limited in scope. If, for example, you go to a magistrates' court for a custody order, then a grandparent can join in the case and ask for access. The divorce court also has power to grant custody to any person – and that probably covers access as well. In all these cases the grandparent must wait for the husband and wife to start the case off before he or she can move in to ask for access. Even if the grandparent did go to court, there is no guarantee that he or she would win; there is obviously a great deal of tension, and a strong case would have to be put forward to satisfy a court that the welfare of the child required grand-parental access.

2 The Cost of Going to Law

My friends tell me that divorce is very expensive. Is that right?

Not necessarily. In the first place you may be able to get legal aid or assistance, and this can reduce the cost to you considerably. Secondly, you can save costs by doing the case on your own without the help of a solicitor. Many people are doing this in straightforward cases. If, however, there is likely to be a dispute over money, the home or the children, then I would strongly advise you to see a solicitor. I will tell you about his charges later in this chapter.

LEGAL AID

Do all solicitors do legal aid work and, if not, how do I find one who will do it?

The answer to your first question is that not all solicitors do legal aid work. If you don't have a solicitor who does legal aid work, then I suggest that you go to your local Citizen's Advice Bureau or town hall and ask to see the legal aid referral lists. These lists are prepared on a geographical basis for the whole of England and Wales and give

1 the names of those firms which undertake legal aid work and

2 the type of work (e.g. divorce, employment, accident cases) which those firms will handle.

I am very nervous about seeing a solicitor because I don't know whether I'll get legal aid until I've seen him and I'm afraid that he might charge me a lot of money for the interview.

I don't think that that is likely to happen. I will try to give you a general idea about the legal aid scheme so that you will know where you stand and understand the questions the solicitor will ask you. If you are in any doubt, ask the solicitor on the telephone how much he will charge for the first interview and tell him that you want to have legal aid.

So how does legal aid work?

Basically there are two schemes: one is called 'legal advice and assistance', and the other is called 'legal aid'. They have many features in common, but there is one big difference: the 'advice and assistance' scheme does not cover the cost of taking any steps in legal proceedings. I might add that the rules are somewhat different in the magistrates' courts where there is a special type of assistance known as 'assistance by way of representation'.

GREEN FORM SCHEME

How do I find out if I can get legal aid for my divorce?

As a general rule legal *aid* is not available for an undefended divorce (and some 98 per cent of all divorce cases are undefended), but you will be entitled to advice and assistance under the so-called Green Form scheme if your income and capital are below a certain amount; you must give the solicitor the necessary financial information, and he will then tell you if you qualify.

What I have said so far relates only to the divorce itself. In the course of the proceedings you may well want to make a number of other claims, and legal aid *is* available (subject to what is said below) for those other claims. The list of matters for which legal aid is available includes the following:

1 a claim for periodical payments;
2 a claim for a capital sum;
3 a claim for a transfer of the house or for a share of the house;
4 an application for an order that your husband leaves the home or stops molesting you, or that you should have the right to live in the house;
5 a claim for custody of, or access to, a child of the family—but only if the claim is likely to be opposed.

Legal aid is also available in those very rare cases where the divorce itself is opposed, and also if you are asking for leave to petition for divorce in the first three years of your marriage. In order to get legal aid for any of the above proceedings (or, indeed, for any proceedings) you must satisfy two conditions. The first is that you qualify financially. The second is that you have a reasonable case.

So, if I want a divorce as well as some money and a transfer of the house, does this mean the divorce will be covered by the 'Green Form' scheme and that the rest of the case will come within the normal legal aid rules?

Yes, that's exactly it. I will explain later (page 40) that under the Green Form scheme you must do some of it by yourself.

DISPOSABLE INCOME AND CAPITAL

Are the financial limits very strict?

The original legal aid scheme was introduced in 1950, and the Government has been criticised many times for not allowing the financial limits to keep pace with inflation (with the result that the proportion of the population eligible for legal aid crashed from 80 per cent in 1950 to only 23 per cent in 1973). Recently there has been some improvement, but there are still far too many people for whom the cost of litigation is a crippling burden and yet for whom legal aid and/or assistance is not available.

Let us look first at legal assistance under the Green Form scheme. You can get this if

1 your 'disposable income' for the seven days up to and including the date of the application does not exceed £85, *or*

2 you are receiving supplementary benefit or family income supplement, *and*

3 in either of the above cases your 'disposable capital' does not exceed £600.

'Disposable income' is worked out by taking all your income and then deducting tax, national insurance contributions and a specified amount in respect of a spouse, dependent children and other dependent relatives. These rules are more stringent than the rules for legal aid because, for example, no deduction is allowed for rent or mortgage payments. Likewise, 'disposable capital' is worked out by taking all your capital and then making a very limited deduction for certain members of the family. One very important point: your 'disposable capital' does *not* include either your home, clothing and household furniture, or the tools of your trade.

I haven't got much money but my wife has inherited quite a lot. Do I have to include her assets in working out my capital?

In a matrimonial dispute the answer is No. You don't have to aggregate the capital and incomes of husband and wife if they are living separate and apart *or* if they have a contrary interest in the matter.

I'm a bit worried about this 'disposable capital' because I've got quite a bit of money in the building society. Could I just give it away?

I'm afraid that the people who drew up the scheme thought of that one. If you get rid of an asset with the intention of thereby reducing your disposable capital you will be assessed on the basis that it still belongs to you.

If I qualify, will I have to pay any money at all for the legal costs of the divorce?

If your disposable income exceeds £40 you will have to pay a 'contribution' towards the costs. The contribution is worked out on a sliding scale. Thus if your disposable income is between £40 and £50 you may have to pay up to £5; if your disposable income is between £80 and £85 you may have to pay up to £49 towards the costs. *The figures given in this paragraph are altered quite often so they may soon be out of date.* Your solilcitor will tell you the latest figures; alternatively you can check up at your local Citizen's Advice Bureau.

So far I have only been dealing with the costs of your own solicitor. If you lose the case, you may also have to pay something towards the cost of your spouse. Normally, however, you won't have to pay very much if you are getting legal aid (see page 49).

What work can my solicitor do for me under the Green Form scheme?

The first point to bear in mind is that he can only incur costs of £75. That won't go very far these days – for most solicitors it represents one or two hours' work. Fortunately the legal aid authorities may (and very often do) allow him or her to go above that limit.

If the solicitor can keep within the costs limit, there are many things that he can do for you under the scheme. Let me list some of them for you:

1 He can advise you whether you have grounds for divorce and whether there are any special problems such as the three-year time limit.

2 He can explain to you the legal effect of a divorce and also what should be done about the children, the home and the family income (including, of course, social security benefits in appropriate cases).

3 He can draft the divorce petition and the statement of arrangements for the children.
4 He can explain what you must do when you file the papers at the court.
5 He can tell you what you must do if you do not know where your husband or wife is living.
6 He can draft the application for directions for trial (see page 72) and the affidavit in support of your petition.
7 He will tell you what you should do when you go to see the judge to talk about your plans for the children (see page 68).
8 He can prepare the application to have the decree nisi made absolute (see page 73).

So what do I have to do by myself?

Anything which involves taking a step in the proceedings. If everything goes smoothly, there are only six things that you will have to do yourself:
1 Sign the divorce petition and the statement of arrangements for the children.
2 File the divorce papers at the court.
3 Swear the affidavit in support of your petition.
4 File the application asking for directions for trial and also the affidavit which you have sworn.
5 Go and see the judge to talk about the children.
6 File the application to make the decree nisi absolute.

You said that legal aid would be available if I had a fight over money, the children or the home. Does it work in the same way as the Green Form scheme?

Basically yes – but there are some differences. First of all, your solicitor cannot decide whether or not you should have legal aid. He can help you to complete a form (for which he can, in appropriate cases, be paid under the Green Form scheme), and this form is in two parts. In one part you must describe your case; this will be looked at by a legal aid committee consisting of practising solicitors and barristers who will decide whether you have a reasonable case. If, to take an extreme example, you are claiming a large capital payment from a husband who is an undischarged bankrupt, legal aid is unlikely to be granted! The other part of the form deals with your financial position, and this goes to the Department of Health and Social Security. They will decide whether your 'disposable income' and 'disposable capital' are within the legal aid limits.

As I have said earlier, the rules for calculating disposable income are more generous than under the Green Form scheme. Deductions are allowed for such things as rent or mortgage interest, rates, repairs and the cost of travelling to and from work.

Can you give me some idea of what I would have to pay if I get legal aid?

At present (1983) legal aid is available if your 'disposable income' does not exceed £4,440, but you may be refused legal aid if your disposable capital exceeds £2,725 and if it appears that you can proceed without legal aid. As a condition of getting legal aid you may have to pay

1 the amount by which your disposable capital exceeds £1,310 and

2 one quarter of the amount by which your disposable income exceeds £1,850.

These figures are regularly revised and can quickly go out of date.

It is important to remember that the figure of 'disposable income' is far less than your actual income. An article in the Law Society Gazette in November 1982 describes how a single parent with three children aged 4, 8 and 13 could get legal aid on a gross annual income of £10,534 and 'free' legal aid on a gross income of £6,304 (or £121.23 per week.)

What happens if I get a rise or win the pools?

You must tell the legal aid committee about it. If the change takes place within twelve months of your legal aid application the DHSS may alter the amount of your contribution and could take away your legal aid altogether if you are no longer eligible for it. Even if the change in your income or capital takes place after this your legal aid can still be cancelled.

EMERGENCY CASES

What about emergency cases?

The legal aid scheme provides for emergency legal aid in appropriate cases; the two obvious examples are domestic violence and child snatching. Such legal aid will usually only last for a short time and will be limited to steps which have to be taken as a matter of urgency. Your solicitor will also complete the usual forms, and your case will be considered in the usual way by the DHSS. If they decide that you don't qualify for legal aid at all, then you will have to pay back all costs incurred on your behalf under the emergency certificate.

BARRISTERS

Are there any cases where I have to have a barrister as well as a solicitor?

Yes, but not many. If a divorce case is defended (and this is extremely rare) it must be heard by a judge in the High Court, and a barrister will have to put your case to the judge. You will not need a barrister if the case is undefended or if the only fight is over money, property or the children. On the other hand your solicitor may recommend that you should have a barrister if the case is complicated or difficult. Barristers are specialists and are generally more experienced than solicitors when it comes to arguing a case in court.

Will my solicitor give me the name of the barrister, or can I choose one myself?

The choice is yours – although obviously your solicitor will advise you. Solicitors work closely with barristers and they will be able to tell you which of them are good for matrimonial work. It's no good getting a barrister who only does property or company work to fight your claim for custody.

Do I have to keep the barrister I choose, or can I change barristers during a case?

You have the right to change barristers, but be careful. Unnecessary changes mean unnecessary costs, and if the legal aid authorities decide that you are running up costs unreasonably, you could get your legal aid stopped.

Is a barrister the same as a QC?

No. A QC (that means 'Queen's Counsel') is a senior barrister who is allowed to put those letters after his name. He must have been dealing with cases for more than ten years and have built up a reputation as a successful barrister. A QC usually charges higher fees than other barristers and normally has another barrister working with him on the case. The use of a QC in matrimonial cases is very rare indeed unless the case is quite exceptionally difficult – perhaps an example might be a money dispute which involves the unravelling of very complicated company accounts.

Will a barrister make the case more expensive?

Not necessarily. The amount of money a solicitor is allowed to charge depends to a large extent on the time he has to spend in dealing with his client's case. If the case is a difficult one, it may in fact be cheaper to go to a barrister to find the answer rather than for the solicitor to do the necessary research himself. After all, the barrister is the specialist and may well be able to find the answer more quickly than the solicitor. In legal aid cases the legal certificate will cover the barrister's fee as well as the solicitor's fee.

THE LAW SOCIETY'S CHARGE

Is the legal aid scheme paid for entirely by the state?

No, there are four other ways in which finance is provided either directly or indirectly. Firstly, we have already seen that you may have to pay a 'contribution' towards your costs (see page 39), and this is paid into the legal aid fund. Secondly, if you win your case, you may be able to get an order for payment of part of your costs by your spouse, and those costs also help to finance the legal aid scheme. Thirdly, in High Court cases your solicitor and barrister have their fees reduced by 10 per cent as their contribution to the scheme. Finally there is what is known as the Law Society's charge. This is very important, and many people do not fully understand just how serious it can be. Your solicitor will tell you about it when you go to see him.

What is the charge, and how does it work?

The charge (which applies in all types of legal aid case and not only divorce cases) gives the Law Society the right to take their costs out of any property which is recovered or preserved in the case for which legal aid has been granted. To see how it works let us take an example:

1 You bring a case asking for the house to be transferred to you. You get legal aid, and your contribution is £100.

2 You get an order that your spouse transfers half of the house to you. The half share is worth £10,000.

3 Your spouse is ordered to pay costs amounting to £1,000.

4 Your solicitor is paid £2,500 out of the legal aid fund.

5 The legal aid fund account looks like this:

Paid out by fund			£2,500
Received by fund	Your contribution	100	
	Costs from spouse	1,000	1,100
	Loss on case		£1,400

The Law Society will therefore have a 'charge' of £1,400 on your share of the house because you have 'recovered' it in the proceedings. When the house is sold the first £1,400 of your share will have to be paid over to the Law Society. Fortunately the money does not have to be paid out straight away, and if you use the sale proceeds of the old house to buy a new house the Law Society may transfer their charge to the new house (this is very important in cases where you need every penny in order to pay for the new house).

The figures in the above example are not too terrible, but sometimes it can be much worse. If, in the above example, your spouse was *not* ordered to pay costs (perhaps because he or she was also receiving legal aid), then the charge would go up from £1,400 to £2,400. If the Law Society paid out another £2,000 under the same legal aid certificate after a hotly fought custody case, the charge would go up to £4,400.

There is, however, an exception in matrimonial cases: the first £2,500 recovered by the legally aided party is not swallowed up by the charge, and maintenance too is not caught by it.

I got an order that my husband should pay me £10,000, and the money has been paid to my solicitor. I need the money to buy a flat, but my solicitor says that I can't have it yet. Why is that?

I think your solicitor is concerned about the Law Society's charge which I have just described. Solicitors are not very keen to part with any money over which the Law Society have a charge; the reason is that they are personally liable for any loss which the legal aid authorities may suffer if they don't get the property to satisfy their claim. He should certainly pay you out the first £2,500 because that is not caught by the charge. Unfortunately it will take some time for the court to work out the sum of money which is payable by the Law Society to your solicitor, and the Law Society will not know the amount of their charge until this has been done. So I'm afraid it could be some months before you will see the rest of your money. You can, of course, ask him to place the money in a special deposit account in your name, so that you can earn interest on it while it is there.

But surely his costs won't be £10,000.

As I have just explained, the Law Society will claim a charge over *all* property (apart from the first £2,500) which is recovered or preserved in the proceedings and will do this until the exact amount of their outlay is known. If your solicitor knows what his charges are going to be, he can give an undertaking to the Law Society that he will not claim from the fund more than a fixed amount. This may help you to see some of your money reasonably quickly. Normally, however, your solicitor will not be able to give that undertaking (and release the surplus money) until his bill has been prepared because he will not know the full extent of his charges until then.

How does my solicitor get paid in a legal aid case?

In some cases the costs will be paid to him by the local legal aid office. This will be so

1 if he is acting for you under the Green Form scheme, or
2 if he is acting for you in the magistrates' court, or
3 if the case comes to an end before anyone has started court proceedings.

In all other cases the solicitor will prepare a very detailed bill setting out his charges. This will then be assessed by a registrar of the court where the order was made (in legal terms the bill is 'taxed', but this has nothing to do with VAT or income tax). The registrar does not have to allow everything the solicitor asks for: in many cases a sum is 'taxed off' the bill, i.e. the bill is cut. When the assessment has been carried out, the registrar will issue a certificate showing the costs which the solicitor can claim from the legal aid fund. Many solicitors are very unhappy about the costs which are payable to them in legal aid cases: often these cases show only a very modest profit or even a loss.

There is one more important point I would like to make. A solicitor acting for you in a legal aid case can get payment only from the legal aid fund. If his bill of £1,000 is reduced by the registrar to £700, he can't ask you to make up any part of the difference.

I want to get a maintenance order against my husband as part of the divorce, but he says that he hasn't got any money and that I should get my money from the DHSS. Can I get legal aid?

On these facts the legal aid committee may well ask you some questions. They will want to be satisfied that your husband has sufficient means to pay and that you have reasonable grounds for seeking an order. If, for example, your husband is unemployed and living on social security payments, it is most unlikely that you would get legal aid for a maintenance claim (because no court is likely to make a maintenance order in your favour). On the other hand, the second ground raised by your husband is *not* a good reason for refusing legal aid.

Can I get legal aid even if I don't want a divorce?

Let's consider three possibilities. Firstly judicial separation: the rules here are the same as for divorce – if the case is undefended you can get Green Form assistance (if you qualify financially), but not legal aid. Secondly proceedings in a magistrates' court: these are covered by a special kind of Green Form assistance ('assistance by way of representation'), but full legal aid is also available if you are outside the Green Form financial limits. Thirdly proceedings in a county court for maintenance or for an order relating to the children: here full legal aid is available in the usual way.

Just one final point: remember that legal aid and/or assistance can be refused if it is unreasonable that you should get it. The Law Society's *Legal Aid Handbook* (1981) says this:

'It might for example be unreasonable for a client who wanted a divorce and whose marriage had irretrievably broken down to apply in the first instance for maintenance in the magistrates' court. Multiplicity of proceedings ought to be avoided.'

If, in your case, you can satisfy the committee that you do not want a divorce then you should be able to get legal aid in the usual way.

I want to get my husband out of the house, but I don't want to go to the local magistrates' court because I've got nasty memories of a recent criminal case. Will the legal aid people make me go there, or can I go to another court?

The legal aid authorities seem to deal with this problem differently in different parts of the country. They want to save money (as we all do), and a case in the magistrates' court will cost them less than the same case in the county court. Now, we saw in the previous chapter (page 23) that either a magistrates' court or a county court can make an order for a husband or wife to leave the home. Many legal aid authorities will say to a solicitor, 'Your client can very quickly get the order she wants from a magistrates' court; we will not let her have legal aid for the county court unless there is some good reason why you can't use the magistrates' court.'

Sometimes the solicitor will be able to say that he can get a better and more effective order from the county court: thus a magistrate can exclude a husband or wife only from the home, but in a county court can exclude the spouse from a given area. In that type of case the committee will grant legal aid for the county court. Whether they will do so in your case is more doubtful; but it is well worth trying, and I think your chances are good.

PROTECTION OF THE UNASSISTED PARTY

My wife will be getting legal aid for this money claim, but I won't. It is going to be very expensive. Can I get anything back if I win?

There are two rules which might help you. Firstly, the court could order your wife (even though she is legally aided) to pay your costs in whole or in part. The snag is that the court will only give you such a sum as it thinks reasonable in the light of your means, her means and the conduct of both of you in connection with the dispute. If, for example, she insists on running up unnecessary costs, then this will obviously be taken into account. Normally, however, you won't get very much.

That leaves the second rule. Even if you are not legally aided the legal aid fund may help you if you win. You will have to show that

1 your wife started the case and

2 the court would have ordered costs against your wife if she had not been getting legal aid and

3 that you will suffer severe financial hardship unless the order is made and

4 that it is just for an order to be made out of the legal aid fund in your favour.

If your wife has no money at all, then I think you could be in difficulties under condition 2, but I think that you should certainly ask for an order. If the court decides all these points in your favour, then you may get the whole or part of your costs paid out of the legal aid fund. Your solicitor will tell you more about it.

If I have to pay something towards my costs, will I get it back if I win?

In some cases, yes. The legal aid office will have your payment (it is known as your 'contribution'), and if you win the case, you may also get an order for costs against your spouse. Now, if these items come to more than the sum paid out by the legal aid office to your solicitor, then you may get some or all of it back. Suppose, for example, you pay £200 towards your costs in a dispute over the home. You win the case, and your spouse is ordered to pay costs amounting to £500. The legal aid office pays your solicitor's bill of £600. They have received £700 and have paid out only £600. They will therefore pay back £100 to you.

COSTS IN NON-LEGAL AID CASES

Can you tell me about the costs of a divorce case if I can't get any form of legal aid or assistance.

The divorce itself will nearly always be undefended and straightforward and will not be very expensive. The problem comes with what lawyers call the 'ancillaries' – disputes over money, the children and the home. In these cases it is vitally important to reach a quick and amicable settlement (the same principle applies in legal aid cases where the proceedings are haunted by the spectre of the Law Society's charge). If you decide that you will fight your husband down to the last plastic toothbrush, then I am afraid that only the lawyers will benefit, and your solicitor's bill could run into several thousands of pounds (a total bill of £15,000 *for each side* is unusual but not unknown). The charges of your solicitor are based on the work he has done, the time spent by him in doing it and a profit element known as 'care and conduct' which is assessed on the time taken and on the complexity of the matter.

When will I have to pay?

This is a matter for agreement between your solicitor and yourself. Many solicitors ask you to pay some money in advance (perhaps £100 or £200, but occasionally more). This is known as 'money on general account of costs and disbursements'. The money remains yours until the solicitor actually spends it on your behalf or until he sends you a bill showing that the actual costs or disbursements are equal to, or greater than, the money you have paid him.

I might also mention something called an 'interim bill'. If the case is going to take a long time, your solicitor can send you an interim bill. You will usually see on it the words 'interim bill' and also a statement that the amount covered by the bill will be reviewed when your solicitor sends you a final bill.

Can I get interest on the money while it is with my solicitor?

You can certainly ask him to put the money in an interest-bearing deposit account so that you can earn interest on it while it is still yours. There are also some cases where your solicitor is under a duty to do this.

What happens if I think that the interim bill is too high?

If the bill contains the words which I have mentioned, then it is called a 'non-statutory bill', and you will have to pay it. If you do not pay the bill, your solicitor will be able to stop acting for you and ask the court to have his name removed from the court record. If you want to change your solicitor, then he will not hand over the papers to you until he has been paid.

Why can't my solicitor wait until the case is over before he sends me a bill?

Because he cannot afford to give you and all the rest of his clients unlimited credit while he has staff to pay, overheads to meet and a family to feed!

What happens when the case is over?

Your solicitor will send you a final bill – it is final because he cannot send you any further bills for the same piece of work.

Can I challenge it?

Yes. Your rights will depend on whether or not court proceedings have been started.

If the whole case has been got rid of by agreement without court proceedings, then we must look at something called a 'remuneration certificate'. Your solicitor must tell you of your right to make him show his bill to the Law Society. They will ask you for your views about the bill and will then issue a 'certificate' allowing the solicitor to charge either the full amount of the bill or a smaller amount. If you are still not happy, then you can insist that your solicitor has his bill 'taxed' (see page 46) by an official at the High Court or the county court (the choice of the court will depend on the amount of the bill).

In the more usual cases where court proceedings have already been started, you can insist that your solicitor has his bill taxed by the court.

Will that cost me a lot of extra money?

Your solicitor will not be very happy at having to spend valuable time and money in preparing a bill for the taxation and will ask the court that you should pay his costs of preparing the papers and coming to court for the taxation appointment. You will have to pay those costs unless you manage to get the bill cut by at least 20 per cent.

Will my solicitor tell me what he will charge?

I would urge you very strongly to talk the matter over with your solicitor when you see him for the first time. Litigation (that means court work) is always a very uncertain business, and in these days of high inflation most solicitors are reluctant to give more than a rough estimate. It may well be that his final bill will be higher than this. You may, for example, start off with what seems to be a simple maintenance claim, and then you may suddenly find that your ex-husband has a stake in a business. This could involve a long and expensive dispute about what the business is really worth and what sums can be raised by your husband without killing the business (in one recent case they spent £12,000 in getting valuations from four accountants, and none of them could agree with any of the others about the value of the business!).

If you are worried about the bill running up (rather like a taxi meter), then you can ask your solicitor to report to you whenever his charges reach a certain amount.

One of the solicitors in the firm is a great expert in divorce cases and usually deals with the big cases that get splashed across the papers. I'm sure he's expensive, and my case should be very straightforward. Can I get someone else in his firm to do it for a smaller fee?

Many firms are very specialized and may have only one person doing divorce work. That person may be

1 a partner in the firm or
2 a qualified solicitor who is not a partner or
3 a legal executive (i.e. a person employed by the firm to work under supervision in a particular field, many of whom are Associates or Fellows of the Institute of Legal Executives).

The firm may also have someone who is training to be a solicitor (an 'articled clerk') who will work under the supervision of a qualified solicitor. These four groups of people – partners, assistant solicitors, legal executives and articled clerks – are known as 'fee earners'.

The firm will have 'expense rates' for each of these four groups on a descending scale through the four groups. The money you will have to pay to your solicitor will depend on which of these four grades is the most appropriate for your type of work. Many solicitors feel very bitter about this; if a bill goes to taxation, the registrar may say, 'This work should have been done by a legal executive.' Many firms cannot afford one at the cost rates allowed on taxation (many registrars allow solicitors only £20 per hour for divorce work, an impossibly low figure for anyone struggling with soaring overheads). So the answer to your question is No, you will not necessarily have to pay for the cost of a very senior specialist if your case can be handled easily by someone who is less experienced in divorce work.

Some solicitors deal with this problem by writing a letter to the client setting out the fee earner who will be dealing with the case and the cost per hour of his or her time. The solicitor will then ask the client to agree to these matters in writing. If you do this, then you will be legally bound by that agreement.

Can I ask my solicitor to do the job for a fixed sum?

Yes. If he agrees to such an arrangement, then it is a binding agreement between both of you. Some solicitors may be reluctant to make such an arrangement because there can so easily be an unexpected complication which will leave him out of pocket.

WHO PAYS THE COSTS?

If my wife goes to court for a divorce, will I have to pay her costs as well as my own?

A lot will depend on the basis of the divorce, and I will deal with this fully in the next chapter. All costs are discretionary, and if your wife wants you to pay the costs, she must ask for this in her divorce petition. The court will hardly ever order costs in a five-year separation case. If the divorce is based on 'two years' separation and consent', then the whole question of costs will usually be dealt with by agreement. If your wife goes for divorce on the basis of adultery, behaviour or desertion, then an order for costs can certainly be (and quite often is) made.

If the court makes me pay the costs of the divorce, will I also have to pay the costs of the disputes over the home and the children?

No. The court will make orders on each separate dispute, and each of these orders will say who has to pay the costs.

My wife is a very spiteful woman and she is threatening to make my girlfriend pay the costs. Can she do so?

Yes. She can go for a divorce on the basis of your adultery with your girlfriend. The girlfriend will be joined in the case as a 'co-respondent', and an order for costs can be made against her if adultery by her is proved. An order is not automatic because, as I have said, the court always has a discretion. If, for example, the adultery was in no way responsible for the breakdown of the marriage, the court may turn down your wife's claim for costs.

COSTS IN DO-IT-YOURSELF CASES

Even if I conduct my own case, it is going to cost me a lot in time and money. Can I get any of it back?

Yes. In legal language you are a 'litigant in person', and the court may, if it thinks fit, order that your costs shall be paid by your spouse. This will give you the right to claim your expenses and the cost of your work in the same way as if you had used a solicitor, but the amount payable in respect of your work is limited to two-thirds of what a solicitor would have got. Also, if the work hasn't caused you to lose any money (such as net wages), you can only claim a maximum of £2 per hour for the work – not very much, but better than nothing.

3 Ending the Marriage

IRRETRIEVABLE BREAKDOWN

I always tell my husband that our marriage is dead, but he never agrees. Is there any chance of my getting a divorce? What do I have to prove?

The Divorce Reform Act 1969 was passed to take the bitterness and hypocrisy out of divorce by sweeping away all the old grounds (adultery, desertion, cruelty, etc.) and replacing them with one single ground – the irretrievable breakdown of the marriage. At the same time Parliament realised that the courts just could not carry out a detailed enquiry into every broken marriage to find out whether the break was irretrievable. So the result was an uneasy compromise. A husband or wife seeking a divorce must prove one or more of five 'facts' as evidence of irretrievable breakdown. So, in your case you must prove that:

1 your husband has committed adultery and you find it intolerable to live with him; or

2 he has behaved in such a way that you cannot reasonably be expected to live with him; or

3 he has deserted you for the past two years; or

4 you have been living apart for the past two years and he agrees to the divorce; or

5 you have been living apart for five years.

If you prove one or more of these facts, you will get a divorce. In theory your husband could produce evidence showing that the marriage has not irretrievably broken down, but in practice this never happens; after all it takes two to make a marriage work.

I might also mention that the duty of proving 'irretrievable breakdown' has been made rather meaningless by the rule (introduced in 1977) that all undefended divorces are to be dealt with under the 'special procedure' without a hearing in court (see page 67).

The divorce law which I have just described is to be found in the Matrimonial Causes Act 1973 which also deals with maintenance, property orders and children.

THREE-YEAR RULE

We have been married for eighteen months, and last week I discovered that when I was on night work nine months ago my wife was having an affair with my best friend. As far as I am concerned the marriage is finished. Can I get a divorce?

You have a problem. The fact that the adultery took place nine months ago doesn't matter because you have only just found out. What does matter is the length of your marriage. The general rule is that you cannot start divorce proceedings until you have been married for three years. There is an exception if you can show that you have suffered exceptional hardship or that your wife has behaved with exceptional depravity; in these cases the court can allow you to bring the proceedings during the three-year period. The courts have become much more willing to allow people to do this in recent years, and if you can show that your health has been badly affected, then leave may well be granted. If you cannot show this, however, it looks as if you will have to wait.

If I do go to court and if the court says I have not suffered 'exceptional hardship', can I start again when the three years are up?

Yes, you can.

ADULTERY

What is the legal definition of adultery? If my husband has sex with his unmarried girlfriend, is that adultery?

The answer to the second question is Yes. Quite a few people seem to think that both parties must be married, but that isn't so. Adultery means voluntary sexual intercourse between two persons of the opposite sex where at least one of them is married, and they are not married to each other.

I can't stand my husband any longer because he has lost all interest in our marriage. I know he has just had an affair with his secretary, but I'm not particularly concerned about that; in fact I have just had an affair myself. Can I get a divorce?

Yes. You can prove the irretrievable breakdown of your marriage by showing that your husband has committed adultery and that you find it intolerable to live with him. The intolerability does not have to be linked with the adultery: they can be quite separate as they obviously are in your case. Just one problem – you cannot rely on his adultery as the basis for a divorce if you go on living together for more than six months after you first found out about it.

BEHAVIOUR

My husband is always drunk, he stays out until one o'clock in the morning and he beats me regularly. I know that he is impossible to live with, but I can't leave the house because I've got nowhere else to go. Can I divorce him because of his behaviour?

You certainly have grounds for divorce because your husband has behaved in such a way that you cannot reasonably be expected to live with him. If you do leave him, you might well be able to get rehoused under the Housing (Homeless Persons) Act 1977 – especially if you have dependent children. If you leave home, then your period of living together will be ignored if it was for six months or less since the last act of misconduct relied upon by you in support of your divorce. If the period of living together was for more than six months, then the court would consider it and the reason for it. You could even get a divorce in a case where you are still living in the same household at the time of the divorce, but you would have to explain the reason for it in your affidavit. The registrar might decide that the case should be heard by a judge in open court.

My wife recently suffered brain damage after a car accident and is behaving very strangely. I am doing my best to put up with it and to help her as much as possible; but there is no sign of improvement, and I think I am heading for a nervous breakdown. Can I get a divorce?

The answer may well be Yes. A lot of people think you can only get a divorce on the 'behaviour' ground if the behaviour is in some way unreasonable or blameworthy, but that is wrong. The Act covers *any* behaviour which makes life together impossible – even if it is caused entirely by illness and is completely blameless. Even under the old divorce law one spouse got a divorce from the other who, because of mental illness, became impossible to live with. The court will have to look at all the facts and must then decide if, after making all due allowances for the illness, it is no longer reasonable to expect you to continue living with your wife. Perhaps an affidavit from your own doctor about your own state of health might help your case.

My husband is completely selfish: he never helps in the house, he is rude to my parents, he hardly ever talks to me and he swears at the children. Whenever I talk to him about a divorce he just shrugs his shoulders and says that I took him for better or for worse and that it is my bad luck that it's turned out worse. Can I get a divorce?

This sounds like a rather 'thin' case, but you might just get by under the 'special procedure' (see page 67). In a divorce petition based on behaviour the conduct must be more than a few minor acts of unkindness, and the court will examine the conduct in the light of your capacity to put up with it. An affidavit from a doctor showing that your health is being affected by the conduct can be useful in a borderline case (and this is clearly such a case).

These allegations about my behaviour are all a pack of lies, and I'm furious. How can I get them thrown out?

You can file a document known as an 'answer' denying the charges, and there will then have to be a hearing before a judge. I fully understand your feelings, but the problem is one of cost. Even if you are financially eligible for legal aid, there is no guarantee that you would get it, and so you could well be facing a bill of several hundred pounds or even more in the unlikely event of the case being fought all the way. In some cases an answer is put in, and then the parties discuss the matter and come to an arrangement. If, for example, your wife has committed adultery, you could file an answer asking for a divorce on the 'adultery and intolerability' ground. You could then try to persuade the other side to let the case go through undefended on that basis.

Some husbands and wives take a different attitude when they recover from the initial shock of seeing the allegations. They say, 'the marriage is dead anyway, and I don't want the aggravation of fighting over the past. I will let the petition go through with a minimum of fuss and publicity and expense, and that will be that.'

DESERTION

What does desertion mean?

Basically it means conduct that brings shared married life to an end. Usually this is done by leaving the home. If your husband just walks out, he will be 'in desertion', provided

1 there was no bargain between you that you should separate and

2 he did not have a good reason for leaving. If, for example, you drove him out because of your nagging or because you refused him sex unreasonably, he will not be in desertion. He could even turn the tables by claiming that you had deserted him by driving him away.

I was very upset when my wife walked out, but now that she has gone I don't find it too bad. Can I divorce her for desertion after two years?

Yes. She left without your consent and so was clearly in desertion at the beginning. Her desertion will continue until something happens to end it – if, for example, she makes a genuine offer to come back or if you enter into an agreement under which you agree to live apart.

My wife moved into a separate bedroom two years ago, and since then we have been leading separate lives. I've now met a girl I want to marry, but my wife isn't very keen on a divorce. Can I get one?

First of all we must consider whether your wife's behaviour will make it possible for you to divorce her on the 'behaviour' ground, and you must give me full details of this. Secondly, it is possible that you can get a divorce on the basis of two years' desertion by her. The main point here is to decide whether you have been living as two households or as one. If the break between you was complete, then you could get a divorce on the basis of desertion provided you can show that

1 you did not separate by agreement and

2 you did not give her just cause for the separation.

If, however, the separation was not complete (if, for example, your wife still did the cooking, shopping, washing or ironing for you), a divorce petition based on desertion may fail.

In practice I suspect that many divorces go through under

the 'special procedure' (see page 67) even in cases where a divorce might be refused if the matter was fully investigated in court.

LIVING TOGETHER

We separated eighteen months ago, but he comes home from time to time and once stayed for a week. We both still want a divorce when the two years are up. Any problems?

It depends on how long in total you have been living together since you separated. You must add up the periods when you have been living together. If they come to more than six months, you do have a problem: any separation before this will be wiped out and will not count. If, however, the periods come to six months or less, they will not stop you getting a divorce, although they will not be counted in working out the two-year period. If, for example, you separated on 1st February 1983, and if you had been together for a total of two months since then, you could file a divorce petition (on the basis of two years' separation and consent) on 1st April 1985.

What about five-year cases?

The same rules apply.

TWO-YEAR SEPARATION AND CONSENT

We split up two years ago because we just couldn't get on, and my wife said that she would agree to a divorce after two years if we hadn't made it up before then. I wrote to her recently and think she may have changed her mind. Can she do this?

I am afraid the answer is Yes. A divorce for two years' separation is only possible if the person asking for a divorce (you, in this case) can prove that the other spouse consents to the divorce at the time she gets the divorce papers. The documents sent to your wife will include an Acknowledgement of

Service form in which she will be asked to say if she consents to the divorce. If she answers 'No', then that will usually be the end of the case. Even if she answers 'Yes' (so that the divorce can go ahead) she can still stop the case by writing to the court withdrawing her consent. She can do this at any time before the decree nisi is pronounced.

FIVE-YEAR SEPARATION

My husband and I have been living apart for the past five years, and he has now met another woman whom he wants to marry. We are both in our late forties, and I am very worried about my financial position (especially as the pension he will be getting from his firm will now go to the other woman). Can I stop him getting a divorce?

When the Divorce Reform Act was going through Parliament many people were worried about what they called a 'Casanova's charter' whereby a husband could leave his wife for a younger woman and then divorce his wife against her will on the basis of five years' separation. To meet these fears two new rules were introduced. These rules apply equally to husbands and wives.

In the first place you may be able to persuade the court to refuse a divorce in a five-year case if you can show that the divorce would cause you grave financial or other hardship and that it would be wrong in all the circumstances to end the marriage. These last words are important because the courts are not very keen to keep alive the empty shell of a broken marriage. If, for example, your husband can show that the social security benefits available to you will largely cancel out the 'grave hardship' which you allege, then a divorce may well be granted. On the other hand the courts might be prepared to refuse a divorce if, for example, your husband is in a position to provide you with compensation for pension loss (perhaps by taking out an endowment policy or deferred annuity for your benefit), and if no such proposals are made; it can certainly be a strong negotiating point.

Secondly, you may be able to ask the court to hold up the divorce in a five-year case (and also in a 'two years with consent' case) until the court has considered your financial position after the divorce. The court will then look at all the relevant facts (including your means, your husband's means and the circumstances which led to the separation) and it will only allow the divorce to be finalized if it is satisfied that

1 your husband should not make any financial provision for you or

2 that the financial provision is reasonable and fair or the best that can be made in the circumstances.

Again, it is useful as a negotiating factor – especially if your husband wants a quick divorce. If, for example, he has promised you the house, you could ask the court to hold up the divorce until the house is actually in your name. Alternatively, the court might allow the divorce to go through in return for an undertaking given by your husband to the court to make such financial provision for you as the court may approve.

VISITORS FROM ABROAD

When I first met my wife we decided to emigrate to Australia and we lived there for five years after our marriage. We've now split up, and I've just come back to England. How long do I have to live here before I can get a divorce?

The English courts can hear a divorce case if

1 you or your wife are domiciled here or

2 either of you has been habitually resident here for one year preceding the start of the proceedings.

By English law a person is 'domiciled' in England if he or she lives here and intends to go on living here indefinitely. In your case it is quite possible that you lost your English domicile when you settled in Australia, but you may well have got it back when you returned. If this is so, you can go for a divorce straight away (assuming that you have got grounds). You should tell your story to a solicitor, who will be able to tell you if you are now domiciled in England.

DIVORCE ABROAD

My husband has left me and gone to live in Canada. I have had a letter saying that he was getting divorced over there. What is my legal position?

If the divorce goes through, you will obviously want to know whether it will be recognised in England as ending your marriage. In many cases the answer is Yes. If, for example, your husband has settled in Canada, he will be 'habitually resident' there, and the Canadian divorce will be recognised as valid over here.

There is, however, a further point. You cannot get a maintenance order or a property order from an English court unless the divorce was granted by a court in this country. If, as seems likely, the Canadian divorce is recognised over here, you cannot get a divorce (or financial orders for yourself) from the English courts because there is no longer any marriage left to dissolve. If you act quickly enough you may be able to get an order from an English court telling your husband not to take any steps in the Canadian proceedings. You can then get a divorce over here, and this will enable the court to make financial orders in your favour.

DIVORCE BY TALAK

My husband is a Pakistani and, when our marriage broke down, went back to Pakistan. I wrote to him to ask him for some money, but he has not sent me anything and says that he has divorced me by what he calls a 'talak'. What is my legal position?

A talak is a type of divorce which is common in some Muslim countries and does not involve any court proceedings. Such a talak may have the effect of ending your marriage, and in that case, as I have explained, you would not be able to get any financial orders for yourself from the English courts. We must find out two things, namely

1 where did the talak divorce take place? and
2 when?

If the talak took place in the British Isles, you needn't worry: you are not divorced. If, however, it took place in Pakistan, then it is almost certain that it will be valid to end your marriage. We must also find out exactly when the talak took place; usually it does not become final for ninety days, and it might just be possible to rush through an English divorce so that you could get a financial support order from the English court (which may be enforceable abroad). You must go to see a solicitor straight away, and he will have to speak to an expert in Pakistani law.

My wife is Italian, and we got married in Italy. Can we get a divorce in England?

The English court can grant you a divorce on the grounds which I have explained (see page 57) if you can show that you are domiciled in England or have been habitually resident here for one year. It does not matter that you and/or your wife are not British subjects nor that you got married abroad. There have even been cases where a divorce has been granted in England even though one of the parties was domiciled in a country which would not recognize the divorce and would regard the couple as still married.

SPECIAL PROCEDURE

I am terrified of having to give evidence in court. Is there any way in which I can be excused?

You needn't worry. The overwhelming majority of divorces go through under what is misleadingly known as the 'special procedure'. In these cases you fill up a form, swear an affidavit and send it to the court. A court official (the registrar) will look at the papers – and especially your petition and the affidavit. If he is satisfied that you have proved your case, he will make a note on the court file and fix a date on which a judge will pronounce the decree nisi of divorce. This will be done in open court, but there is no need for you to be present.

I should perhaps add that if there are children, the court will make an appointment for you and your husband to see the judge in his private room so that he can make sure that the arrangements for the children are satisfactory.

Do the solicitors also come along to these appointments?

It is not necessary for them to do so, and in legal aid cases the cost of attending is not covered by the Green Form scheme. In a recent survey involving 1,500 parents only 22 per cent were represented. The hearing is informal, and the survey showed that having a lawyer there did not affect the actual result of any particular case.

How do I start getting a divorce without using a solicitor? Where do I have to go?

There are a large number of county courts in England and Wales, and many of these are 'divorce county courts', meaning that divorce cases can be dealt with there. You can use *any* divorce county court and not just the court of the district where either of you lives.

To start the case off you have to prepare a document called a 'petition'. This is not as frightening as it sounds because forms can be bought from a law stationer and may also be available from the court. You must then fill in the blanks on the form – where and when you were married, where you lived, the names and ages of any children of the family, details of any previous legal disputes and so on. A number of different forms are available (some for husbands, some for wives) depending on the basis for the divorce (behaviour, desertion, etc.), and you must be careful to choose the right form. You will normally need at least three copies – one for you to keep, one for the court to keep and one for the court to send to your spouse. If there are children of the family under 16 (and sometimes even over 16), you must also complete (with the same copies as before) a form called 'statement of arrangements for children' in which you give details of what your proposals are.

When you have completed these two forms you hand them in, or post them, to the court together with your marriage certificate and a fee of £40 (no fee is payable if you are on supplementary benefit or family income supplement or on Green Form assistance).

THE UNNAMED ADULTERER

My husband says he has committed adultery, but he won't tell me the woman's name because he doesn't want her involved in the divorce. What happens in a case like that?

Normally the other party to the adultery must be named in the petition. He or she must be made a 'co-respondent', and the court will send him or her a copy of the petition. In your case, however, you must say in your petition that your husband committed adultery with a person whose identity is unknown to you. If there is enough evidence of the adultery (and it is usually provided by a confession statement) then a divorce can be granted.

NON-DISCLOSURE OF ADDRESS

I am terrified of my husband and don't want him to find out where I am living. Do I have to give my address in the divorce petition?

No. You can leave the address out and you (or your solicitor) can then go to see the registrar at the court and explain the position to him. He may sometimes ask you to swear an affidavit setting out the special circumstances of your case. If he believes what you tell him, he may very well allow the divorce petition to go ahead – even though the address is not included. That, of course, is not the end of the matter. There will be a number of affidavits and other documents in the course of the case, and you must make quite sure that your address does not appear in any of them. It may also be important to draw up the 'statement of arrangements for children' carefully. If it gives the name of your children's school, for example, your husband may be able to trace your address either directly or indirectly from the school.

MISSING SPOUSES

My wife and I have lost contact with each other since we split up. I gave the court her last known address, but the envelope came back marked 'Gone away'. Can I still get a divorce?

Yes. The next step is to swear an affidavit which is then sent to the court. The affidavit must describe in detail what steps you have taken to trace your wife – perhaps by contacting relatives, friends, neighbours, trade unions, clubs, employers, the telephone directory or in any other way. If you happen to have her national insurance number, it may be possible to get the address from the DHSS, but only the court can do this. The registrar may ask you to come and see him at the court so that he can ask you about your enquiries. If he is satisfied that you have made all reasonable enquiries, he will make one of two possible orders. He may well tell you to have the petition advertised in a newspaper – but only if he thinks there is a fair chance your wife will see it. Alternatively he may allow the case to go ahead even though your wife has not received the papers: in legal language, he may make an order dispensing with service on her.

GETTING DIVORCE PAPERS

I handed in the divorce papers to the court, and they said that they would send the papers to my husband. Last night he rang me up to say that he had torn up the petition and that he wouldn't take any part in the case. What happens in a case like that?

The court must be satisfied that the papers have been received. What normally happens is that the person receiving the papers will sign the 'Acknowledgement of Service' (see page 63) and send it back to the court. This is not absolutely necessary and you can swear an affidavit describing the telephone call. The registrar may then say that he is satisfied your husband has received the papers, and the case can then go ahead.

I haven't heard from my wife for six months, and then yesterday I suddenly got some divorce papers from the court. What should I do now?

It is always advisable to see a solicitor who can advise you on all aspects of the case – the conduct of the divorce itself, children, your home, money, tax and so on. If you don't want to see a solicitor, you should read very carefully the papers which you have received and especially the form headed 'Notice of Proceedings'. This explains the various options available to you and some of the legal effects of a divorce. After reading this form and your wife's petition you should complete the form headed 'Acknowledgement of Service', sign it and send it to the court.

THE NEXT STAGE

I have filed my divorce petition at the court, and the court have told me that copies have been received by my husband and by the other woman. What happens next?

Let me assume that your case, like 98 per cent of all divorce cases, will go through undefended. You can tell that by looking at the answer to question 4 on the Acknowledgement of Service form: 'Do you intend to defend the case?'

If your husband's answer to that question is 'No', the case will be one for the 'special procedure' (or, as it is commonly known, 'divorce by post'). In that case you send to the court a form of 'Request for Directions for Trial' in which you will ask for the case to be dealt with under the special procedure. You will also have to swear an affidavit and send that to the court at the same time. The affidavit (see below) starts by asking you to answer a number of questions, and then you must swear that your answers are true. Also, if your spouse has sent the court a signed Acknowledgement of Service form, you must identify his or her signature on that form.

Now let us look at the very occasional case where the question in the Acknowledgement of Service form, 'Do you intend to defend the case?, produces the answer 'Yes'. Your spouse will then have to file an 'answer', usually within 29 days of receiving the petition. The case will then go to the High Court (but not necessarily the High Court in London) and be heard by a judge.

What are the questions in the affidavit?

I have explained earlier (see page 57) that there were five 'facts' for a divorce – adultery, behaviour, etc. Each of these has a separate affidavit, and the questions are not difficult to answer. Thus, for example, question 3 of the adultery affidavit reads:

'State briefly your reasons for saying that the respondent has committed the adultery alleged.'

The answer in many cases will be:

'See confession statement attached to this affidavit.'

Question 5 is even more straightforward. It asks:

'Do you find it intolerable to live with the respondent?'

If you are going for a divorce based on desertion or separation, you must say when the separation started. In all cases your right to a divorce may be affected by periods of living together, and you must give details of any such times in your affidavit.

DECREE NISI

The court has sent me a form called a 'decree nisi'. Does that mean that I am divorced?

No. A divorce is granted in two stages. The first stage is the decree nisi which is made by the judge in court. Later the court will grant a 'decree absolute', and it is this decree which ends your marriage.

DECREE ABSOLUTE

What do I have to do to get this decree absolute, and how long do I have to wait?

The decree nisi will have a date on it, and normally the decree absolute cannot be made until six weeks have passed since the decree nisi. Shortly before the six weeks are up you can fill in a simple form asking for the decree nisi to be made absolute, and you then send that form to the court. The court will then make the decree absolute and send copies to yourself and to your spouse.

You have just said that it 'normally' takes six weeks. Can I get it sooner?

Yes. The six-week period can be cut down, but you will have to go to a judge to explain the reasons why you want this.

The court may, for example, shorten the six-week period if the wife is expecting a child by another man and wants to marry the father of the child before the child is born.

I got a decree nisi of divorce on the grounds of my husband's behaviour, but then we got together again. Things went quite well for a time, but now I've decided that it won't work out. Can I still get a divorce?

If you have lived together for not more than six months since the last act relied upon, this can be ignored, and you can apply for the decree nisi to be made absolute in the normal way. If, however, you have lived together for more than six months (even after decree nisi), the court will have to look into this to see whether you can reasonably be expected to live with your spouse. These are the two basic rules, but there is also a third rule which is sometimes overlooked. This says you have to make a special application to the court if your decree nisi was granted more than twelve months ago. You will then have to explain the delay, and the court may either allow the divorce to go through or it may cancel the decree nisi altogether.

What about those awful cases I read about in the papers?

Divorce cases only get reported if they are 'defended' cases; very few cases are defended, and of these not very many are newsworthy. You might, for example, have a husband and wife who feel they need to get rid of their frustrations (and their sense of failure) by making allegations against each other. Or a wife might make allegations that the husband totally denies. Finally you might hear of cases where each party agrees that the marriage has irretrievably broken down, but for a different reason.

The procedure in defended cases is slightly more formal. The case starts, as before, with a petition. The other spouse (the respondent) then sends an 'answer' to the court, and the original petitioner can then send an answer to the answer; this is known as a reply. When this has been done, the petitioner or the respondent asks the court registrar to make arrangements for the trial and must say where he or she wants the case to be heard. The husband and wife may not be able to agree on the place for trial, and the registrar will then have to decide for them.

The main difference between defended and undefended cases is that defended cases take place in open court – in the High Court, either in London or at any of the branches, called District Registries, round the country. There will be a judge (but no jury), and unless you conduct your own case you will have to have both a solicitor and a barrister to represent you. The case will proceed in the same way as any other High Court case. All documents in your possession relating to the case must be disclosed to your spouse, and he or she is entitled to see them – except for letters, etc., between you and your legal advisers. The petitioner will give evidence and will then be asked questions by the barrister acting for the respondent. When the petitioner's evidence is completed, the respondent will give the other side of the story and then be asked questions by the petitioner's barrister. At the end each barrister will summarize the case on behalf of his client, and the judge will then decide the case. He may grant a decree nisi to the petitioner, or to the respondent, or to both of them, or (very occasionally) to neither.

A defended divorce can be long, painful and expensive, and should be avoided if at all possible.

NULLITY

What is a decree of nullity?

It is a decree of the court which recognizes that the marriage has failed because of some legal defect which existed at the date of the marriage or by reason of wilful refusal to consummate it. The marriage may be either void or voidable. If it is *void* there has never been a marriage at all; if it is *voidable* the marriage can be ended by the decree of the court. There is a decree nisi and a decree absolute in the same way as for divorce.

NON-CONSUMMATION

I feel terribly frustrated because the sexual side of our marriage has been a disaster. What is the legal position?

We must consider whether your marriage has ever been consummated at all. Consummation is only effected by full penetration. If this is not possible, or if one party wilfully refuses to consummate the marriage, then a decree of nullity can be obtained; on the other hand, the fact that the husband is unable to ejaculate, or is sterile, is not of itself a ground for ending the marriage. If there has been consummation, then the mere fact that a husband and wife are not sexually compatible is not of itself a ground for divorce or nullity (although in very many cases it is the true reason for marriage breakdown).

A refusal of sexual intercourse can, in appropriate cases, form the basis of a divorce petition on the behaviour ground.

PREGNANCY

We have lived together for a year, and we got married five months ago when my wife was pregnant. When the child was born I realised that it wasn't mine. Can I get a divorce?

No, but you can get a decree of nullity. The marriage is 'voidable', and a decree which ends a voidable marriage has the same effect as a decree of divorce. There is a time limit: you must present your petition to the court not later than three years from the date of the marriage.

VENEREAL DISEASE

My husband is suffering from venereal disease. Is this a ground for divorce?

If he was already suffering from it when you got married, you may be able to get a decree of *nullity*; the rules are similar to those set out in the previous answer. If he contracted it after you got married, then this is evidence of adultery which can, of course, be linked to intolerability as the basis for a divorce. Finally, if he insists on intercourse while knowingly suffering from the disease, you can obviously divorce him on the 'behaviour' ground.

PRESUMPTION OF DEATH

My first husband left me a long time ago, and I couldn't find him anywhere. Ten years later I met my present husband, and we got married. I described myself as a widow when we went to the registry office. Now, to my absolute horror, my first husband has reappeared. Can my second husband divorce me?

He can't divorce you because you have never been married to him! There is a rule that a person is presumed to have died if

1 he or she has been missing for seven years and
2 nothing has been heard from him or her and
3 all due enquiries have been made.

In this situation the spouse of the missing person might want to marry again; the second marriage would be valid – unless the missing spouse chose to spoil it all by turning up! This has happened in your case, and so I am sorry to say that your second marriage is completely null and void. Either you or your second husband could petition to the court for a decree of nullity on the grounds that you were already married at the time of your second marriage. The decree of the court would confirm that the marriage is null and void.

What about money?

In the nullity proceedings the court can make the same money orders as on divorce.

All this is very messy – could I have done anything to make the second marriage completely safe?

Yes. If there are reasonable grounds for believing a husband or wife to be dead, the court can grant a decree of presumption of death and dissolution. You would have had to show reasonable grounds for belief in your husband's death, but absence for seven years will often be good enough.

Once the court grants you a decree absolute of presumption

of death and dissolution, you can get married again in exactly the same way as if you had been divorced. If he turns up later, the validity of your second marriage would not be affected in any way.

If I want to go on living with my second husband, can I divorce my first one?

Yes – on the grounds of five years' separation.

Could I get money from my first husband in that sort of case?

As you have remarried without divorcing your first husband I am afraid the answer is No. The right to claim maintenance, a lump sum or a property order on a divorce (or on a decree of presumption of death and dissolution) is not available to a husband or wife who has 'remarried'. This includes not only a valid remarriage, but also a remarriage which, as in your case, is null and void.

VOID MARRIAGES

Are there any other cases where a marriage is null and void?

Yes, there are five other cases.

1 A marriage is void if either party is under sixteen.

2 A marriage is void if both parties are male or if both of them are female.

3 A marriage is void if the husband and wife are within the so-called 'prohibited degrees' – in other words if they are closely related either by blood or by marriage.

4 A marriage is void if at least one party is domiciled in England, and the marriage was polygamous.

5 A marriage is sometimes void if the necessary legal formalities have not been carried out.

This reference to polygamous marriages sounds interesting. How many wives can I have?

If you are domiciled in England (see page 65), then I am afraid you can have only one wife at a time.

A friend of mine recently brought his wife with him from abroad. The marriage broke down, and he left his wife and married another woman in a registry office. Is his second marriage valid?

No. First of all, your friend may find himself in trouble if he made a false statement to the marriage registrar. Secondly, the second marriage is void because your friend was a married man. Thirdly, the first wife can divorce your friend either on the basis of his behaviour (see page 59) or because of his adultery, i.e. sexual intercourse with his so-called second 'wife'.

I came to England from Nigeria with two wives and am now fed up with both of them. How does English divorce law deal with a case like this?

The rules which I have described earlier in this chapter apply to both of your marriages. At one time the English courts could not deal with polygamous marriages at all; but they were given the right to do so in 1972, and now the normal rules will apply. Your solicitor will want evidence from an expert in Nigerian law that both marriages are valid.

What happens if I marry a third wife in England?

You will not be able to get a licence to marry. All marriages in England are monogamous, and you, as a married man, will not be able to enter into a monogamous marriage.

4 Money, Property and Housing

POWERS OF THE COURT

What sort of orders can the court make on a divorce?

Since 1971 the courts have had very wide powers indeed to readjust the income and the capital of a divorcing couple. They can order any or all of the following:

1 periodical payments,
2 a lump sum or sums,
3 a transfer of property,
4 a settlement of property,
5 the variation of a settlement or
6 a secured provision.

SETTLEMENT

You say that the court can order a 'settlement of property'. What does that mean?

Basically, it means an order under which different people have rights over the property at different times. Perhaps the most common example is the order which says that

1 the ex-wife shall have the right to live in the house until the youngest child is eighteen, and
2 after this has happened the house is to be sold, and the proceeds split.

What does the 'variation of a settlement' mean?

It means that the courts can rewrite the terms of a settlement which the husband or the wife or someone else (such as a parent) has made for the benefit of one or both of them. If, for example, Albert takes out an insurance policy on trust for his wife, but she is not named in the policy, such a policy could be for the benefit of any woman who happens to be Albert's wife when he dies. If Albert's wife Jane divorces him the court can rewrite the policy in such a way that only Jane can benefit.

Some wealthy families draw up what are called 'marriage settlements' – although this is becoming less common than previously. In these settlements the parents provide money for the benefit of the couple and the children. Even though the money comes from the parents the court can rewrite the terms of the deed – something which the parents will not feel very happy about.

Can a parent take away this power of the court to rewrite the trusts?

Yes. If the trust deed says that it shall automatically come to an end as soon as a divorce petition is filed, then there is nothing the court can do about it. Whether the parent would want to go that far is another matter, and there could also be tax complications in that sort of case.

We are getting divorced, and my husband says he will pay me £10 per week and that he can't afford any more. I can't live on that. How much will I get if the case goes to court?

It is impossible to answer this question precisely. Section 25 of the Matrimonial Causes Act 1973 lays down some guidelines, but the courts have said time and again that each case turns on its own facts and that there is no formula which will cover every case. This, of course, makes it very difficult to give accurate advice: in one case the judge said that it was all a question of trial, error and imagination (which isn't very helpful).

Anyway, the guidelines which the court must consider include the following:

1 your income and capital and that of your husband;
2 your obligations and those of your husband;
3 the length of your marriage;
4 the standard of living which you enjoyed before the breakdown;
5 any illness or disability;
6 the contributions made by your husband and yourself towards the welfare of the family;
7 any benefit, such as a pension, which is lost on divorce.

After looking at all these factors, the court must try to put you in the same position as if your marriage had not broken down, insofar as it is practicable and (having regard to your conduct) just to do so. This is a highly controversial matter, and many people think that the law is out of date and should be changed. A Bill to cut down the duty to pay maintenance after divorce failed to get a second reading on 4th February 1983, but it may well come up again before long.

ONE-THIRD?

Doesn't a wife always get a third of the husband's income?

No. As I said in my previous answer there is no precise mathematical formula. Nevertheless, the courts and advisers must start from somewhere, and so *as a starting point* the courts often take a figure which will bring the wife's total income up to one-third of the joint incomes. So if the husband is earning £9600 and the wife £2400, the one-third starting point would give the wife an order of £1600 per annum. The court will then look at the figures in the light of the needs of the parties and will decide whether the suggested order is a reasonable one or whether some adjustment is required.

Is the one-third gross or net?

The starting point is to take gross figures – although national insurance contributions and the cost of travelling to work can be deducted (and perhaps also the cost of employing a child-minder). When this has been done the court will stand back and consider broadly the overall *net effect* of the order on the parties – is it too high, too low or just right? The impact of tax will be considered at this stage; in many cases the one-third starting point does not produce the right result, and an adjustment will then be made.

It is all very unscientific, but the court is often faced with an impossible task (spreading one income between two families), and it must try to get as near as possible to a reasonable result.

How widespread is this one-third rule?

The courts have said many times that it is not a 'rule', but only a guideline or starting point. In a 1982 case the court said that it wasn't very helpful in cases involving very large or very small sums of money, but it could still be useful for the cases in between.

How does the court work out the 'net effect' of an order?

Basically they take the husband's gross income (generally larger than the wife's) and deduct

1 national insurance contributions,
2 the amount of the order and
3 any tax payable on the husband's income having regard to the order.

The court then carries out a similar exercise for the wife's income (with the order being added rather than taken away). When this has been done the court will consider the expenses of each party (and in particular their housing costs) and will ask whether the net effect of the order is reasonable or whether adjustments are required.

How does child maintenance fit in?

If the registrar does operate the one-third starting point, he will usually take one-third for the wife, and he will then decide on the right amount for the children having regard to their needs. He will then consider the 'net effect' of the orders in the way that I have described.

What about school fees?

If the husband and wife had agreed that the children would have private education, the court will sometimes deduct the cost of these fees before they work out the one-third.

Will the wife also get one-third of the capital assets?

No. Each case will turn on its own facts, and there is no 'one-third' starting point. The court must look at the seven guidelines which I mentioned in a previous answer (see page 83). The reasonable requirements of the wife must be balanced against the husband's ability to pay.

Can you give me an example of how these cases work?

Yes. Let us look at the case of Mr and Mrs Potter which was heard by the Court of Appeal in June 1982. It was a fairly short (six-year) childless marriage. Both Mr and Mrs Potter worked, and when they got divorced neither of them claimed periodical payments from each other. Mr Potter had capital assets of £60,000; most of this was locked up in a busines which had a strong cash position. Mrs Potter had capital assets of £8,400 and a half share in the home, but her income was not large enough to meet her living expenses. The three members of the court gave Mrs Potter £10,000. The income from this would enable her to make ends meet, and Mr Potter would be able to raise that sum without difficulty.

INVESTMENTS

When I got married I had investments worth £20,000 – they were transferred to me by my first husband as part of a divorce settlement. It now looks as though my second marriage is also going to end in divorce. Will my husband be able to claim a share of my investments?

The seven guidelines which I mentioned earlier (see page 83) include the 'financial resources' which the husband and wife have, or are likely to have, in the foreseeable future. Many of the cases are concerned with 'family assets' such as the house, the car and the furniture, but the court has very wide powers indeed over *all* types of property including a business, investments, gifts from parents and grandparents and even money received as accident compensation. In the case of Dennis v. Dennis in 1975 the father of Mr Dennis gave a farm to his son after he had separated from Mrs Dennis. The court treated the farm as one of the assets of Mr Dennis and ordered him to pay a lump sum to his wife.

WILLS OF LIVING PERSONS

My wife is an only child. Her father is in his seventies, and his health is not good. He is a rich man. Can I ask him to tell the court about his will?

This very problem arose in a case in 1977 involving a Mr and Mrs Morgan. The judge said that the evidence of Mrs Morgan's father would certainly be useful and important, *but* he also ruled that the father could not be compelled to tell the court what he was going to do in his will. This was a matter which he could decide for himself, and his privacy must be respected.

My former wife's boyfriend is a very successful businessman. Can I find out how much he is worth? I don't see why I should have to pay anything for her because she is being looked after by him.

The money which he makes available to your former wife is a 'resource' of hers which must be taken into account. The boyfriend himself cannot be ordered to file an affidavit, but

1 he can be ordered to attend court to answer questions and to produce any documents; and/or

2 your wife can be asked to deal with his financial contribution in her affidavit; if her affidavit is evasive or incomplete, then you can ask the court to draw the obvious conclusions.

I married my husband soon after his divorce, and his former wife is now bringing a claim for maintenance and for a lump sum. Do I have to be involved in those proceedings?

The court has power to make you come along to the hearing so that you can be asked questions; and they can also order you to produce documents.

My friends tell me that most of my salary will go to support my husband's former wife. Why should I have to do that?

There has been a great deal of criticism of the present law from persons in your position, and a change may be on the way; but the split of one income between two families is a difficult and largely insoluble problem. The law requires the court to consider the 'resources' and 'obligations' of your husband and his former wife. Now, if you were not working, then your husband's obligations to you and to any children of your marriage would clearly affect the amount of money which, in realistic terms, is available to support his former wife. If, however, you do work, then your contribution to the family budget will release more of your husband's money for the support of his former wife.

Is it a very big problem?

There is no agreement about this. A pressure group called Justice in Divorce has claimed that the present law causes very great hardship to husbands and second wives, but a recent survey carried out in Oxford points to a very different picture (see an article in *The Guardian* on 3 September 1982 at page 3). This survey looked at 217 divorced women and found that only two of them were receiving maintenance for themselves. Some others received maintenance for children, but no less than nine out of ten received, in total, less than £10 per week. The authors of the survey say that 'the "meal-ticket for life" myth seems to bear very little relation to reality. The women in this study worked during marriage, over half worked during separation and divorce and are working now whether or not they have re-married.'

What about my capital? Can my husband's former wife take that as well?

No. If, however, you make your capital freely available to your husband, this could be taken into account. In one case, for example, a husband ran a company which was owned by his mistress and had a completely free hand to draw out what he wanted. The court said that this had to be taken into account in deciding what he could afford to pay by way of maintenance. The judge said, 'whether or not he is on her board, he is in her bed and in her pocket.'

CLEAN BREAK

I'm quite happy to pay my former wife £20,000 towards a house and to give her most of the furniture, but I want that to be in final settlement of all claims. Can I do that?

This is a question which many husbands ask, and the courts have considered it in a number of recent cases. They have said that where a marriage is dead the parties should be strongly encouraged, in suitable cases, to make a clean break. Unfortunately, they have also said that such an arrangement will only work if the husband and wife come to an agreement about it.

How does it work?

I said earlier (page 15) that an agreement to take a sum in full and final settlement is not legally binding. The position is different, however, where you have a court order. What happens is that, by consent, your wife's maintenance application will be formally dismissed by the registrar, and that will be that. It is important, however, that you disclose your true financial position and do not mislead your wife in any way (see page 153).

You said that a clean break was a good idea 'in suitable cases'. What does that mean?

First of all, you are under a duty to support your children, and this is not cut down in any way by a divorce. Obviously you cannot get rid of that duty either by an agreement or in any other way. Secondly, a clean break is not suitable where the parties are on very low incomes and where either or both of them are living on social security.

SHORT MARRIAGE

Our marriage was a disaster, and we split up after only eighteen months. Do I have to pay her any money on divorce?

Before answering that question I must have some further details. How old are you, and how old is your wife? Are you both working? Is there a child? Did your wife give up any property or money (such as a flat or widow's pension) when you got married? If you are both young, healthy, childless and working, you can argue very strongly that you should not have to pay maintenance to your former wife, and the court may well agree with you.

LIVING TOGETHER BEFORE MARRIAGE

We lived together for five years before we got married, but we have now split up. How will this affect my money claims on a divorce?

The real question here is to find out what contribution you have made to the welfare of the family both before and after the marriage took place. We must then decide whether your pre-marital contribution will count in your favour. The courts have not always agreed with each other on this point, but I think that they will increasingly take it into account – especially if there are children. In one case decided in 1980 the parties had lived together for twenty-four years before their very short marriage, and the wife had devoted a great deal of time and energy to bringing up a child and to helping to build up the family business. On these facts the judge decided that it was clearly right and just to take her contribution into account. If the marriage had continued, the husband would have given some capital to his wife, and the court awarded her a capital sum on the divorce.

SHOULD THE WIFE WORK?

My wife wants me to go on supporting her after the divorce, but I think that she should go out to work. What will the court decide on this?

I must obviously start by asking whether any work is available. After all with unemployment at its present high rate your question could well be academic. If work is available, we must look at other factors. The Matrimonial Causes Act

1973 says that the Court must take into account 'the earning capacity . . . which each of the parties to the marriage has or is likely to have in the foreseeable future'. In practice registrars' attitudes vary quite a lot. If your wife is in her mid fifties, say, or disabled, or if she has to look after very young children, then almost certainly she will not be expected to try to find a job. On the other hand a young and childless woman will be expected to do so. The difficult area is that of a youngish woman with two children aged perhaps eleven and nine. I think that the majority of registrars would take the view that she should try to get a job provided, of course, that satisfactory arrangements could be made for the children.

I have never worked during our marriage. Why should I start now just because my husband has left me?

This is the other side of the same coin, and, as I have said, the attitudes of different registrars do vary. They are, of course, under a duty to restore the parties to their pre-breakdown position if this is both practicable and just. At the same time some registrars clearly take the view that marriage should not be a mealticket for life. A recent survey highlights these differences. One registrar said this:

'If she had not got a job and the husband says it is easy for her to go out and get money, I would say, "Did you marry her with a view to her going out to work to supplement the family income?" If not, she would get an order because you cannot expect her to do it now. Even if only 25 or 30 she would get an order.'

Another registrar took a different view. He said, 'Even if the wife has never worked, I would say, "Why shouldn't she?" and unless there is some reason on the grounds of health or otherwise, then she should work.'

My wife is a successful businesswoman and runs a farm said to be worth about £200,000. I can only work part-time because I had a serious accident some years ago. Now, after ten years of marriage, my wife has told me that she has fallen in love with a neighbour and that she wants a divorce. My financial position is obviously very bad. Can I get a large sum of money from her on the divorce?

Let me say first of all that the rules governing maintenance and property orders on divorce make no distinction between the sexes: there is complete equality as to their rights and duties. There have been relatively few cases where such orders have been made against wives, but that is because, in the vast majority of cases, the wife has been the economically weaker partner. In your case, however, your wife is obviously in a far stronger financial position than you are, and this fact, coupled with your disability, gives you a strong claim to a lump sum payment when the court is reallocating family assets on a divorce.

There is, however, one further point to consider. Where assets are locked up in a business, the courts are very reluctant to make a lump sum payment which will have the effect of crippling the business – of killing the goose that lays the golden egg. We must also look closely at the true value of the farm; the figure of £200,000 is a paper figure based on the value of the farm as a going concern and bears no relationship to what the business would fetch if it had to be broken up. In other words, there is no comparison between, say, a business worth £200,000 and investments of that amount. If you cannot come to an agreement with your wife, you will have to show that the sum which you require *can* be raised by her (whether by borrowing, or by selling part of the farm or otherwise) without crippling the business.

When we first split up I went along to the magistrates' court, and my husband was ordered to pay me £10 per week. I've now decided that I want a divorce. What happens to the magistrates' order?

It will carry on until
1 it is brought to an end by the court or
2 you remarry after the divorce or
3 either of you dies.

In other words, it won't automatically come to an end on the divorce. You will have to give details of the magistrates' order in your divorce petition.

Should I get the magistrates' order cancelled?

Only if you think that you can get a better order from the divorce court. If, for example, your husband has capital assets, the divorce court can give you extra protection by making an order for a 'secured provision' (see below). Also I think I can safely say that magistrates tend to think in lower terms than divorce court registrars.

This last point is not always very important because many divorce court orders are registered in magistrates' courts (see page 156), and a husband may then ask for the order to be reduced. If the order remains in the magistrates' court, the money will be payable through the court, and the clerk can chase up the husband if he defaults.

How do I get the order cancelled?

Either by going back to the magistrates or by asking the divorce court to do it when they are dealing with your case.

Can I get an increase in the order after the divorce?

Yes, this is possible if you can show that the increase is justified.

SECURED PROVISION

I want an order for periodical payments, but I'm worried that he won't pay. Is there any way of making sure that I get my money?

Yes. If your husband has capital assets, then the court can order what is known as a 'secured provision'. He is ordered to transfer assets to trustees; they will pay the income from those assets (for example, dividends on shares) to him while he keeps up his maintenance payments. If he defaults on his maintenance, the trustees can pay the income direct to you. Finally, if that income does not cover the maintenance, the trustees can sell the assets.

This seems to be a very useful sort of order.

It is – but only if the assets are there. I might just mention two other advantages. First, secured provision can be 'assigned'; in other words it can be transferred to someone else (perhaps a bank as security for your overdraft). In practice, however, I don't think that many people will regard it as a good security – after all, the divorce court may vary it if circumstances change. Secondly, it can last longer than an unsecured maintenance order. A normal maintenance order automatically ends if either you or your former husband dies; if, however, the court orders a secured provision for you, this can go on even after your husband's death.

What happens if I marry again?

Both types of order will automatically come to an end.

MAKING THE CLAIM

I am going to divorce my husband. How do I set about claiming money from him for my support?

Basically your divorce petition will have a list of all the things that you are claiming – periodical payments, a transfer of the house and so on. Later on you send him a form saying that you want the claim to go ahead. He will then have to send to the court an 'affidavit' – a statement sworn in front of a solicitor – setting out his income, his capital, his debts and so on. When this has been done your solicitor will go through it with you and will prepare an affidavit for you to swear. In that affidavit you can deal with your own financial position and also make comments about his affidavit. If, for example, he says that he has no money at all, you could point out that he runs a very expensive car and that he always has a summer holiday in the South of France and a winter ski-ing holiday in Switzerland. This may produce further affidavits from him and so on.

When the affidavits have been sworn and filed, the case will be heard by a court official called a registrar. He will read the affidavits, listen to the lawyers on both sides and then make an order.

Will it be necessary for me to go to court?

That depends on the registrar. Some like to have the husband and wife there, but others don't. Your solicitor will tell you about this before the case is heard.

What happens if the registrar makes an order which I find unfair?

You can appeal against the order to a judge. This will, of course, increase the expense, and your solicitor will have to advise you not only about the costs, but also about the chances of getting the order changed.

INTERIM ORDER

I am sure my husband is earning a lot of money, but he just won't turn up at court or file a proper affidavit. What should I do?

I suggest you get your solicitor to prepare an affidavit for you to swear. In this you can say not only what you earn, but also what you think your husband earns. The registrar can then be asked to make a temporary order (known as an 'interim order') based on what you have told him. Hopefully this will bring your husband to his senses, and he will then tell the court what the true position is.

SECRET REMARRIAGE

On the divorce I gave her the house and £10,000 (which I couldn't really afford) because I thought she needed it. I've just heard from a friend that she has just married a very rich surgeon. I think she must have been planning to get married again while we were sorting out the property, but she never said a word about it: she just said, 'Let's have a clean break', or something like that. I'm furious – can I get it back?

You may be in difficulties here, but I must have some further details. Did she actually say that she wasn't planning to remarry? If she said that, then you could go to the court and try to get the transfer set aside. Did she file any affidavits? Was she asked to file any affidavits? Once you get to the affidavit stage, there must be full disclosure, and your chances of success are good. If, however, you merely negotiated and then asked the court to, in effect, 'rubber-stamp' your agreement, it seems that there was no duty on your wife to disclose her remarriage plans, and the financial agreement which you have made cannot be changed.

COMPANY ACCOUNTS

I work as a company director, and my wife and I are getting divorced. She is asking for periodical payments and a lump sum, and her solicitor wants me to produce the company records over the past five years. The divorce is a private matter between my wife and myself, and I don't see why the company should be involved. What happens if I refuse to produce the documents?

Your wife will ask the registrar to make an order for production.

Will he make it?

This depends on your relationship with the company, and there are three possible situations.

1 If you own all the shares (or nearly all the shares), then the registrar is likely to make an order for production (he will regard the company realistically as you under another name) if he thinks that production is necessary to decide the case or to save costs.

2 If you are only a minority shareholder, you should tell the registrar that you cannot produce the books without the consent of your fellow directors and that this is likely to be refused. In this sort of case the registrar will almost certainly not make an order.

3 If you are a majority shareholder, but if somebody else owns a large minority (perhaps 30–40 per cent), then the registrar will have to perform a balancing act in deciding whether or not to order production. He must balance the hardship to your wife of *refusing* production against the hardship to yourself and your fellow directors and shareholders of *ordering* it.

Can he order the company or my co-director to produce them?

A recent case says that the court can authorise a document known as a 'subpoena' to be sent to a person who is not involved in the case, and this document can require him to bring documents to court. Your wife would, of course, have to show some good reason before a subpoena will be issued by the court. In the recent case she had grounds for believing that the husband had made payments to his business associates so as to reduce his assets.

My husband works for a company, and I'm sure that a lot of his expenses are paid for by the company. What sort of documents can I ask him to produce?

Apart from standard items such as bank statements and tax returns, you should ask him to produce all bills, invoices, credit card accounts, receipts and other vouchers relating to entertainment, air fares, holidays, hotels, restaurants, night clubs, home decoration and repairs, clothing, jewellery and all other expenses which he has incurred (whether in his own name or in the company's name) for himself, his wife, his children or other persons over a specified period (perhaps two or three years). If he refuses to produce these vouchers then you can apply to the registrar, and he can order production.

CONDUCT

My wife has never looked after me properly. She has refused to have sex with me since our daughter was born and now she has left me for no apparent reason. I am filing the divorce papers and I have told her that she is not getting a penny from me. Can she take me to court?

This is an area of law about which husbands feel very bitter and in which the practice of the law may be a long way ahead of public opinion. In practice the wife's conduct (in the sense of misconduct) will seldom reduce the award; it will only do so if it is 'gross and obvious'. There are two main reasons for this. Firstly, the courts are not equipped to carry out a detailed investigation into conduct because this would involve delving into the whole history of the marriage (one judge used to say that it always takes three to commit adultery). Secondly, it is the policy of the law to take the heat and bitterness out of divorce so far as is possible, and this object would clearly be defeated if maintenance applications were used by husbands and wives giving vent to their frustrations and counter-allegations about who did what to whom. Nevertheless in extreme cases the court may decide that the wife's conduct was wholly or mainly responsible for the breakdown, and in that case her maintenance will be reduced. In a recent non-divorce case a magistrates' court awarded Mrs Robinson only one-eighth of Mr Robinson's income after finding that his conduct was in no way responsible for her decision to leave him. She appealed to the High Court, but she lost her appeal. There is of course no guarantee that a divorce registrar would approach your case in the same way. Each case turns on its own facts, but many registrars are reluctant to become involved with conduct.

If we have a fight about my wife's conduct will that make the case more expensive?

Yes, because the registrar will have to transfer the case to the High Court and it will have to be heard by a judge. It will also take a lot longer than fifteen minutes – which is the average time of a hearing before a registrar in a dispute over money.

Can you give me some examples of cases where a wife has had her maintenance cut because of her conduct?

As I have said the cases are very much the exception rather than the rule. Here are some examples:

1 In the case of Cuzner v. Underdown in 1974 the wife allowed the husband to transfer the house into their joint names without telling him that she was committing adultery and that she was going to leave him. The court did not think much of the wife's behaviour and ordered that her half share should be wiped out.

2 In the same year the court had to consider the case of Mr and Mrs Armstrong – a case in which the husband was never the same again after his wife had shot him! When she claimed a financial order on divorce she was awarded £1 per year by way of periodical payments and only a quarter of the husband's capital assets.

3 In 1977 the court considered the remarkable case of Mr and Mrs West. The 'marriage' in that case had lasted for some six years, but it didn't amount to very much because Mrs West refused to set up home with Mr West. They only stayed together for occasional weekends (during which two children were born!). The court found that the reason for Mrs West's behaviour was her reluctance to leave her parents. Even though she may have been morally blameless, that, said the court, didn't matter. Mrs West's conduct had clearly been 'gross and obvious', and her financial order was fixed at £550 per year – this being one-eighth of their joint incomes. She appealed against this order, but she lost her appeal.

Can the court increase the maintenance because of the husband's bad behaviour?

Yes – but again only in exceptional cases. In 1974 the marriage of Mr and Mrs Dixon came to an end after Mr Dixon had committed adultery with his daughter-in-law. The judge described the conduct as shocking and ordered Mr Dixon (a farmer) to pay a lump sum which was rather larger than he would otherwise have been ordered to pay. In the following year the court gave the home to Mrs Jones after Mr Jones (who was in prison) had assaulted his wife with a knife and injured her wrist so badly that she had to give up work. (Incidentally the assault in that case took place after the decree absolute of divorce, but that didn't matter). Finally, in 1976 we had a rather different situation. In that case Mr Martin took the family assets and squandered them on a number of unsuccessful business ventures. The court held that he had had more than his share of the family assets. He was ordered to transfer his interest in a farm to Mrs Martin and also to pay her a lump sum.

LUMP SUM ORDER

My husband has offered me £5,000 as part of a divorce settlement and says he can't afford any more. That's probably true, but I know that he will be coming into a lot of money under a trust when his mother dies. If I take the £5,000 now, can I come back for more later?

It is almost certain that any arrangements will be embodied in an order of the court, and on that basis the answer to your question is No. The divorce court cannot alter a lump sum order, nor can they grant you a second lump sum. The best solution is to find out how much he is going to inherit and then to ask the court to make an appropriate order and to postpone the date for payment until the trust money falls in.

STANDARD OF LIVING

When we got married we had a very poor standard of living because all the money was ploughed back into my husband's business. I also worked in it until our first child was born. He is now a millionaire and last year sold out to a public company. He has now told me that he is going to emigrate with his secretary and has offered to pay me £50,000 in full and final settlement if I will divorce him. What should I do?

The first thing to do is to make sure that your husband does not transfer all his assets abroad (if he has not already done so). You can bring a claim against your husband for maintenance or for a property order or for a lump sum (either in a divorce petition or separately) and at the same time you can ask for an order stopping him from transferring his assets abroad. You would have to satisfy the court that he intends to defeat your claim, but on these facts this should not be too difficult.

Turning now to the case itself, it is obvious that the figure of £50,000 is far too low and a poor reward for all your efforts. The court does have very wide powers, and this is one of the very few cases where these powers can be used to the full. I obviously can't tell you how much you will get, but you might be interested to hear about a 1981 case where the facts were quite similar to yours. In that case the husband's realisable assets were valued at £23 million, and he also earned a salary of £44,000 per annum in Jersey. The wife had made a major contribution to the husband's business success during a marriage which had lasted for twenty-four years, but at the time of the divorce her only asset was her share in the home valued at £50,000. The judge awarded her a lump sum of £600,000 on the basis that she was now entitled to enjoy a very high income after tax and a very high standard of living. Not surprisingly, the husband took the case to an appeal court, but they refused to reduce the lump sum. They said that £600,000 was probably too high a figure, but it was within the area of reasonable disagreement, and they would not say that it was actually wrong. This case is not a legal precedent, but it shows how the courts deal with very exceptional cases such as yours.

THE HOME – WHAT CAN BE DONE?

Shortly after we split up my husband came to see me and got me to make over the house to him. We are getting divorced now, and I rather wish I hadn't done it. Can I ask the court to let me have it back?

You can certainly try but there is no guarantee that you would succeed. Your strongest arguments would be to show that

1 at the time of the transfer you were under great emotional stress and

2 you did not have independent legal advice.

If you can go further and show that the transfer was made under some sort of threat, then I think that your chances are very good indeed; but if there were no threats, then it might be more difficult. In one recent case Mrs Backhouse left Mr Backhouse because she had fallen in love with another man. Later she transferred her share in the house to Mr Backhouse out of, as the judge said, a sense of guilt. She then asked the court for a transfer of property order and a lump sum order. The judge held that:

1 the transfer should be ignored;
2 her conduct should not be ignored; and
3 a small lump sum of £3,500 should be paid to her.

Our home is in joint names, and my former husband wants it sold. I need the house so that I can bring up our three children there. Will it have to be sold? Can I get it transferred to me? What do the courts do in cases like this?

The courts will do everything possible to prevent a sale unless there is no viable alternative. If, for example, it is clear that, even with help from the DHSS, neither party will be able to keep up the mortgage, then a sale may well be the only solution. The courts will consider the overriding question of housing needs – especially the housing needs of the children. The courts exercise their wide discretionary powers in a number of different ways, and in your case the court can make at least four possible orders (apart from immediate sale). First, they may order a transfer into your name in return for a reduction in periodical payments – especially if your husband tends to default on his payments. Secondly, they can order you to buy him out – perhaps with a lump sum payable by instalments. Thirdly, they can give the house to you and give your husband a 'deferred charge' – a charge which is not to be enforced until you move out or until the youngest child completes fulltime education. Fourthly, there could be an order for a 'deferred sale'. In many cases, however, immediate adjustment is better than a deferred order: the trouble with a deferred order is that the eventual proceeds of a sale will not be enough to provide housing for either or both of you, and you may by that time be too old for a new mortgage.

I want to go on living in the house for the time being, but I may well want to move in four or five years time. Will I be able to do that?

This should be possible if the matter can be agreed or if you can satisfy the court that you should be given that right. If the house becomes yours on the divorce, you can live in the house until you want to move and then sell it. If, however, your husband wants to keep some interest in the house (for example, a share of the money when the house is sold), then the order will have to be drawn up very carefully to give you what you want. The big question is likely to be one of money; if you do decide to move, will you have the necessary cash to pay removal expenses, estate agents' fees, legal fees, stamp duty, furnishing expenses and a new mortgage? If you can afford to take out an endowment policy, that would be a useful way of providing a capital sum to cover some or all of these expenses.

I have never worked during our marriage, and my husband says that he is going to sell the house and that there is nothing that I can do to stop him. Is he right?

No. We must first have a look at the deeds of the house to see if the house is in his name or in your joint names. A recent survey suggests that three out of every four houses bought by married couples are bought in joint names. If this is so in your case, you are in no danger because the house cannot be sold without your signing the transfer form. If the house is in your husband's name, you can protect your right to go on living there by registering what is known as a Class F land charge (if the land is unregistered) or a notice (if the land is registered). This is fairly straightforward and will bring your rights of occupation to the notice of anyone who wants to buy the house. The practical result will be to freeze any sale. If you don't know whether the land is registered or unregistered, a solicitor can find out for you; it is important to use the right form of registration because you could lose your home if you get it wrong.

COUNCIL HOUSING

We live in a council house, and my husband is the tenant. He has now left me, and we are getting divorced. Can I go on living in the house?

The answer may well be Yes (if you can pay the rent). Your husband will probably have what is called a 'secure tenancy' which means that the council can't turn him out unless the court makes an order for possession. Such an order can only be made on certain grounds (such as non-payment of rent), and in a number of cases the court must be satisfied that it is reasonable to make an order. He does not lose his rights merely by leaving the house if you are still living there as his wife (the position changes after a divorce). If the council do take proceedings, you can ask the court to adjourn the proceedings or to postpone the date of possession.

When the divorce comes through you can apply for an order transferring the tenancy to you. There is, of course, no guarantee that the court will make such an order, and it will want to know whether the council is in agreement.

If the council does not make a transfer order on the divorce, you have no right to go on living in the house, and your husband, as the tenant, can turn you out. In such a case the council may well be under a duty to rehouse you under the Housing (Homeless Persons) Act 1977 (see page 26).

CAN I PAY THE RENT?

If he doesn't pay the rent, can I pay it?

If you are living in the house as a wife (i.e. before the divorce), the landlord is bound to accept rent from you even though your husband is the tenant.

This rule applies to private landlords as well as council landlords and is a very important safeguard. You should tell the landlord to let you know straightaway if the rent falls into arrears.

Once you are divorced, your right to pay the rent and to resist the landlord's claim for possession comes to an end unless the divorce court transfers the tenancy into your name.

MORTGAGES

The house is in my husband's name; but he has left, and I don't know where he is. What happens if he gets into arrears with the mortgage? Can the building society turn me out?

If you have registered your right of occupation (see page 104), the building society must let you know that they are asking for possession of the house. You will normally be able to take part in the case and may be able to stop the building society taking over if you can show that you can pay off the arrears.

This is the main problem: the building society are *not* bound to tell you that the arrears are piling up, and so by the time it gets to court it may be impossible for you to find the money to pay off the arrears.

The right to pay instalments and to take part in the case will end on a divorce unless your rights of occupation have been extended by the divorce court.

When we got married I paid the deposit on the house and also paid for central heating, but the house was put in my husband's name. We paid off the mortgage two years ago, but last year my husband mortgaged the house again (this time to a different building society) to pay for an extension to his business showroom. I knew nothing about all this until yesterday when my husband told me that he hadn't repaid the mortgage and that he was leaving me because he wanted to get away from it all. Can I legally stay in the house?

Yes. The law will treat you as a part-owner of the house because of the money you put in. As you were living in the house when it was mortgaged last year, the building society will be legally bound by your rights. This means, for example, that they won't be able to sell the house without your permission.

SHOULD SHE PAY ME RENT?

The house is mine, but my ex-wife wants a right to live there for the rest of her life. Why should she live there rent free?

A good question. The courts have recently started ordering the ex-wife to pay what is called an 'occupational rent' in that sort of case. Once again, however, the court will have to ask whether the ex-wife can afford to pay such a rent – although, presumably, supplementary benefit would be available for it.

What will the rent be, and will I have to pay tax on it?

The registrar will have to fix what he considers to be a reasonable market figure. There may also be cases where the payment of rent will be postponed until, for example, the mortgage has been paid off or until the children are off the wife's hands. In these cases the registrar will not fix the rent until the time comes for it to be paid.

As far as tax is concerned I'm afraid that the answer is Yes – but not on all of it. You will be able to claim tax deduction for money spent by you on maintenance, repairs, insurance and rates.

The house is a very small one and is mortgaged up to the hilt. Neither of us could afford a new home out of the proceeds. Couldn't we just ask the court to order a sale so that the local authority would have to step in to rehouse us?

This argument was put before the court by a Mr Harvey in 1981, but the court didn't like the idea at all. The judge said: 'There is a matrimonial home, and at least one party can be housed; and if that can be done, doing justice to both parties within the terms of [the Matrimonial Causes Act], that is a course which the court ought to take.'

I suffer from a heart condition and, if my wife gets the house, I'm thinking of moving down to Brighton. Will I be able to get a council flat there?

I have already mentioned that if you want accommodation under the Housing (Homeless Persons) Act 1977 you have to clear a number of hurdles (see page 26). Firstly, you must prove that you are homeless or that you are threatened with homelessness. Secondly, you must prove that the homelessness is unintentional (and eviction under a court order will satisfy that test). Thirdly, you must have a 'priority need': perhaps your heart condition (making you, in the words of the Act, 'vulnerable') may help you to clear this particular hurdle. A letter from your doctor would obviously help.

There is one further point – do you have any local connection with Brighton? Will you have a job there? Do you have family there? If the answer is No, then the council may be able to pass the buck to a housing authority in another area where you do have a local connection. So I suppose that it would be advisable to try to get a job there first.

DEFEATING THE WIFE'S CLAIM

I asked my husband if I was going to get the house: he said that he had made the house over to his company and that the company had given a mortgage over all its property to the bank. Where does that leave me?

I'm afraid your position is not a strong one. The court can set aside the transfer to the company if this was done in order to defeat your rights, *but* this won't help you as against the bank if they took the mortgage in good faith without knowledge of your claim. In other words, you may end up getting a mortgaged house.

DAMAGES

I am having an affair with a very rich man, and my husband is now threatening to sue him for thousands of pounds. Can he do so?

No. At one time a husband could sue a co-respondent for damages for adultery, but those claims were abolished in 1970. If your husband petitions for divorce, he may get an order for costs against the co-respondent; but the costs of the divorce itself are unlikely to be very great.

EVICTION

When you were dealing with the breakdown of the marriage, you told me that the court could turn me out of my own home. Can the court do that even after a divorce?

The court has a power and a duty to protect children and can turn you out of your home if this is necessary to protect the children. This could be done if, for example, you, your ex-wife and the children are still living in the same house after the divorce and if your presence is in some way harmful to the children.

If there are no children in the house, or if they have all reached eighteen, then the general power of the court to turn you out of your own home will no longer be available.

What happens if my ex-wife asks the court to transfer the house to her?

If the court makes an order under the Matrimonial Causes Act 1973, it can decide who shall live in the house. Also, if the house is transferred into the name of your wife, she can ask you to leave (with the help of the court if you refuse) because your right to live there as a husband came to an end on the divorce.

5 Tax and Social Security

VOLUNTARY MAINTENANCE

My husband has left me. He says he will try to send me about £40 per week and so far he has paid it regularly. He says that he doesn't want a formal separation and he doesn't want to go to court. Will I have to pay tax on the money that I get?

No. Tax is payable on maintenance paid under a court order or under an agreement, but not on maintenance which is paid under the loose type of arrangement which operates in your case. I might just mention that your husband would actually be better off from a tax point of view if he did make the payments under an agreement or court order. In that case he would get tax relief on the payments at his top rate of tax. If, however, he merely carries on with the informal arrangement, he will get no tax relief at all (although he may be able to claim the higher married man's personal allowance which is not normally available where a husband and wife are living apart). In a sense that is not your problem; but if you point it out to him, he might be prepared to increase the payments on the basis that he will still be better off than he is at present.

GROSS OR NET?

The court has made an order that my husband must pay me £40 per week. Will that be gross or net?

If the order says nothing about tax, it will be an order to pay the specified amount 'less tax'. This means that your husband will deduct tax when he makes each payment. As I mentioned in a previous answer (page 21) there are some orders which are paid gross. These are known as small maintenance payments, and the amounts are varied from time to time. At present an order in favour of a spouse is payable gross as a small maintenance payment if it does not exceed £33 per week or £143 per month. Any larger order is paid net.

How much tax is deducted from each payment?

Your husband will deduct tax at the basic rate (for 1982–3 this is 30 per cent).

TAX REPAYMENT

Can I get the tax back?

Yes – if your personal reliefs and allowances allow you to do so. Your husband will (or should) send you a certificate of deduction of tax, and you can use that certificate to get a repayment in appropriate cases.

Can you give me an example of how this works?

Yes. For the purposes of this example we will assume that

1 you earn £1,000 from a part-time job,

2 your husband is ordered to pay you £40 per week (£2,080 per year) for the support of yourself and the child of the marriage, and

3 the tax rates and allowances are those in force for 1982–3.

On these facts you will fill in your tax return showing the gross amount of your salary and the gross amount of the maintenance. You are entitled to a single person's allowance of £1,565 and (assuming that the child is living with you) you are also entitled to a 'single parent' allowance of £880. The calculation would be as follows:

Income	Salary		£1,000.00
	Maintenance		2,080.00
	Total		£3,080.00
Reliefs	Personal	£1,565.00	
	Single Parent	880.00	£2,445.00
Taxable			£ 635.00
Tax on this @ 30%			190.50
Tax deducted from maintenance (£2,080.00 × 30%)			624.00
Tax overpayment (repayable) £624.00 – £190.50			£ 433.50

Can I still claim the £1,565 personal allowance if I go to live with my boyfriend?

Yes.

In your calculation you gave a figure of £880 for the child. What happens if there is more than one child?

I am afraid that there is no increase in the relief.

My ex-husband has said that he wants some of the relief because his tax rate is higher than mine. Can we agree that he should have it? What happens if we can't agree?

The relief is available if a child is *resident* with the taxpayer for the whole or part of the tax year. So, if the children spent part of the year (perhaps school holidays or weekends) living with your ex-husband, he will be able to claim part of the relief. In this situation the relief will be split between you as you may agree, and if you cannot agree, the Inland Revenue will split the allowance on a time basis. If, therefore, the children spend nine months of the year with you and three months with their father, you will get £660 and he will get £220.

How does child benefit and one-parent benefit fit into all this?

They do not come into the calculations because they are tax-free payments.

How would the above calculation work out if the payments were small maintenance payments?

It works the same way. Your income will be the salary and the maintenance; from this you deduct the allowance of £2,445, and any balance will be taxed. The only difference is that you do not reclaim tax in respect of the maintenance because none has been deducted.

Can the court ever order a tax-free amount?

Yes, but it is fairly rare. If, for example, you wanted a fixed sum of £50 per week to meet your expenses, you could ask the court to award you 'such sum as after deducting tax at the basic rate shall equal £2,600 per year payable weekly'. In this case the £2,600 would be a net amount; the gross sum is approximately £3,714, and your ex-husband would get tax relief on that gross amount.

In your calculation you referred to a tax repayment. Does that mean that I have to wait until the end of the tax year before I can get the tax back?

In theory, yes; in practice you may be able to persuade the Inland Revenue to allow your ex-husband to make gross payments. This is often possible if you can satisfy the Revenue that you will have a tax repayment claim. Such an arrangement will be a convenient short cut; instead of paying the tax to the Revenue (who repay it to you) your ex-husband will pay it straight to you.

I am prepared to pay £60 per week to my former wife and £20 per week to each of my two children – they are 11 and 9 and live with my ex-wife. My income from my company is £20,000, and I pay mortgage interest of £2,000. Could you please tell me how the maintenance affects my tax?

Yes. I will assume that the payments are going to be made under a court order. Your personal tax will look like this:

Income			£20,000.00
Deductions and Reliefs			
	Mortgage interest	£2,000.00	
	Maintenance	5,200.00	7,200.00
			£12,800.00
	Personal allowance		1,565.00
Taxable			£11,235.00
	Tax on this @ 30%		£3,370.50

You will see that the maintenance has completely wiped out your liability to higher-rate tax.

Now, in addition to your *personal* tax as set out above, you may also have to pay some tax on the maintenance (which you will get back by deducting it from the maintenance payments). The position will depend once again on whether the payments are 'small maintenance payments', and on your figures the position is as follows:

1 £60 per week to your former wife is *not* a small maintenance payment. Therefore you will have to pay to the Inland Revenue tax at the basic rate on the annual amount:

(£60 per week × 52 × 30%) = £936

You will send your wife a certificate of deduction of tax and also her *net* weekly payments of:

£60 – (£60 × 30%) = £42

2 I said earlier that a court order payment for a spouse or former spouse was payable gross as a 'small maintenance

payment' if it did not exceed £33 per week or £143 per month. A similar ceiling covers payments for the maintenance of persons under 21. So the payments to each of your children can be made gross, and you will not have to account for any tax on them.

AGREEMENTS AND ORDERS

Why do you keep referring to court orders? Surely I could get the same tax relief if I merely asked my lawyer to draw up an agreement?

No. If you agree to pay money direct to your unmarried child under 18, the tax rules say that the income is taxed as if it was still yours. The only exception is where the payments are made under a court order; even here you could find yourself involved in a dispute with the Inland Revenue (although usually there is no problem).

ORDERS FOR CHILDREN

Is the wording of the order important?

Yes. You must make it perfectly clear that the money is to be paid *to* the children (although in practice they would be paid to your former wife who would be able to give you a receipt for them). If the order were to provide for payment to her of '£60 per month for herself and £20 per week for each child', the tax position would be very different. First of all, the 'small maintenance payments' ceiling in this situation is only £18 per week or £78 per month – so that the payments may have to be paid net. Secondly, the tax effect of the order at the receiving end will be much worse.

Why is that?

Basically, because the whole £100 per week would be taxed as the income of your former wife, and even if she had no other income, there could well be a substantial tax bill:

Income (maintenance)		£5,200.00
Reliefs (personal and single parent)		2,445.00
Taxable		£2,755.00
Tax on this @ 30%	=	£ 826.50

Now contrast that with the previous order – £60 to your former wife and £20 to each child. The essential point to grasp is that each child has its own personal allowance of £1,565, *and this should not be wasted.* The tax computation would be:

1	Your former wife	
	Income	£3,120.00
	Reliefs	2,445.00
	Taxable	£ 675.00
	Tax on this at 30%	£ 202.50
2	Each child	
	Income	£1,040.00
	Personal relief	1,565.00
	Tax	Nil

You can see from this figures that the wording of the order has resulted in a tax saving of some £624. Further savings are possible by using the children's reliefs to the full. If, for example, an order was made for payment of £47 per week to your former wife and £26.50 per week to each child, no tax at all would be payable!

SCHOOL FEES

My wife and I are about to get divorced. I want to get tax relief on my children's school fees and I also want to make sure that the money goes straight to the school and not to my wife. Is this legally possible?

Yes, but the procedure is absurdly technical and highly artificial. There has to be a court order whereby you pay a periodic sum to each child (this cuts down your tax bill because the income which you use to make these payments is treated as being no longer yours). Then, the child has to make an agreement with the school and under that agreement

1 the school agrees to educate the child;
2 the child agrees to pay the fees;
3 the child appoints the headmaster or bursar as its agent to receive the maintenance money from you; and
4 the school agrees to use that money to pay the fees.

The court order has to be worded in a special way to make the arrangement tax-effective. All this is fairly new, and I imagine that your children will not be slow to exploit their newfound bargaining power!

WHO SHOULD PAY THE BILLS?

I am quite prepared to allow my former wife to live in our former home and I will go on paying the rates and other outgoings. Is this tax-effective?

No. You will not get tax relief on the rates and other outgoings which you pay even if you agree with your former wife that you will pay them. It would be more tax-efficient to increase the periodical payments so that your former wife can pay them. This will only be so, however, if her income, including the higher periodical payments, is taxed at a lower rate than yours. It may also be necessary to adjust the amount year by year because rate bills, etc., are never static.

Can't we just have an index-linked order?

Not all registrars are very keen on the idea, and I'm not entirely sure whether it can be done. The order would have to be very carefully worded – and in any event you would have to be quite sure you could afford it!

TAX AND THE MORTGAGE

I am offering to transfer the house to my former wife, and I will keep up the mortgage repayments. Will I still get tax relief on the interest?

No. Mortgage interest relief is only available if at the time of payment you own an interest in the house. If therefore you transfer the house to your former wife, the relief will be lost.

The house is, in fact, in joint names, and so presumably I can still get tax relief if I just leave it in joint names and allow my former wife to go on living there.

Yes – but there is a snag. As you still own the house there could be mortgage interest problems when you buy a new house. At present relief is only available on loans of up to £25,000, and this will have been used up by the house in which your former wife is living. In other words you will not get further tax relief on the interest on your new house.

So what is the solution?

The solution is similar to the one which I suggested when dealing with rates (see above). If you can make the necessary arrangements with the building society (and they may require a guarantee from you), you could transfer your share to your former wife and increase the periodical payments to enable her to pay off the mortgage. You would then get full tax relief on the payments (including the capital repayment element) and could also get mortgage interest tax relief on your new home in the usual way. Your former wife would have quite a high taxable income, but the mortgage interest tax relief would reduce her tax burden.

The house is in my husband's name and he has walked out. Will I get tax relief if I pay the mortgage?

In theory – no, because the house isn't yours. In practice the Inland Revenue will usually allow relief in this sort of case. Get in touch with your local Inspector straight away and explain the position to him.

DIVORCE SETTLEMENTS AND CAPITAL GAINS TAX

My wife and I split up four years ago, and we are now getting divorced. She and our son have been living in our former home which we brought ten years ago in our joint names for £20,000. I also lived there until I left four years ago. My wife now wants to move to another part of the country. She has suggested that we should sell the house and that I should transfer my share to her as part of a divorce settlement. The house has now doubled in value. What is the capital gains tax position on my share if I agree to my wife's suggestion?

Capital gains tax is payable at 30 per cent on chargeable gains. In this case the gain may be as high as £20,000 (net proceeds of sale less purchase price). £10,000 of this will be your gain and taxable unless an exemption applies. Perhaps the most important exemption (and one that clearly applies in your case) is the 'principal residence' exemption. In this case the house was your principle residence for six of the ten years, and that slice (i.e. 6/10ths) will be exempt. You can also treat the last twenty-four months in the same way. This brings the exempt slice up to 8/10ths, i.e. £8,000. The balance of £2,000 will come within your annual exemption of £5,000 (as increased by annual index linking) and if that exemption has not been used up by other gains then no tax at all will be payable.

I have divorced my wife, and we are still arguing about what is going to happen to the house in which she is living. In the meantime I have bought another house for myself and my new wife, but I may have to sell it in a few years time because we are thinking of emigrating. Will I get capital gains tax relief on both houses?

You cannot get relief on more than one house for any one period of ownership. If the house where your wife was living was also your own principal residence, you can of course claim the exemption for that period (and also for the last twenty-four months of ownership).

There is also a special rule which applies where a house is transferred to your wife as part of a divorce settlement. If your wife has been living in the house as her principal residence ever since you left, the Inland Revenue allow you to treat *her* occupation as if it had been *your* occupation so that complete exemption will be available for you. There is, however, a snag – you cannot claim this special relief if you have already told the Revenue that your new house is your principal residence. Also, if you do claim the special relief for the old house, you will lose some of the relief for the new house. It is a complicated business, but your solicitor will advise you as to what you should do.

Just one final point: the special rule I have described applies only if the property is transferred to your former wife. It does not apply if the property is sold and the proceeds are then divided between you.

My wife's solicitors have said that she needs a capital sum of £10,000 so that she can pay the deposit on a house and furnish it. If I pay this sum to her, will I have to pay capital gains tax?

Capital gains tax is not payable on cash; so if you happen to have the cash available, no tax problem will arise. If, however, you have to sell investments in order to raise the £10,000, then capital gains tax will be charged on any gain which you may make on such a sale.

I recently read an article in the paper about a husband who was proposing to give a holiday home to his wife as part of a divorce settlement. I think it said that capital gains tax could be avoided if the transfer took place within twelve months of the separation. Is that right?

Not entirely. On the facts of this case we need not consider the 'principal residence' exemption. We must therefore look at another rule – namely, transfers as between husband and wife. It is here that the timing of the transfer can be important. If the transfer takes place in the tax year (April 6th to April 5th) in which the separation takes place, the person who makes the transfer (in this case the husband) will not have to pay capital gains tax. That can be good news for him – but it's not so good for his wife. In this situation he is treated as transferring the house to his wife for a sum equal to the sum for which he bought it. So suppose he bought it in 1970 at a cost of £10,000. It is now worth £25,000. They split up in July and the transfer takes place in November. The Inland Revenue will treat the husband as having transferred the house to his wife for £10,000. If she sells it for £30,000 her taxable gain will be £30,000 – £10,000 = £20,000 (although the whole or part of that gain would be exempt if she moved into the house as her principle residence).

If the transfer did not take place until the following May (ten months after the separation but *not* in the same tax year), then the above rule would not apply. The husband would be treated as transferring the asset at its true value of £25,000 (and would therefore have made a large chargeable gain), and the wife would also be treated as acquiring it for £25,000. I might add that if she moves into the house as her principal residence, the principal residence exemption would apply to any gain made by her.

DIVORCE SETTLEMENTS AND CAPITAL TRANSFER TAX

Do the same rules apply for capital transfer tax?

No. The rules for capital transfer tax are entirely different. This tax is charged if a disposition reduces the value of a person's estate; thus property which is transferred as part of a divorce settlement could, in theory, be caught (but see below). Also, there is no exemption for a principal residence. In practice, however, this tax is unlikely to be a problem on a divorce settlement, and there are three reasons for this. In the first place any transfer between husband and wife (whether living together or apart) is not a chargeable transfer. Secondly, a transfer for the maintenance of a former spouse on a divorce is similarly non-chargeable. Finally, the tax will not catch a transfer which is not intended to provide what is called a 'gratuitous benefit'. This means that if the husband transfers property as part of a court order, or as part of a compromise of court proceedings, there will be no charge to capital transfer tax.

If, for some reason, it is felt that there might be a tax risk, the only completely safe way of avoiding tax is to hold up the decree absolute until the transfer has been made.

MAINTENANCE AND SUPPLEMENTARY BENEFIT

We are getting divorced, and there is not much money to go round. My wife is getting supplementary benefit. Why should I have to work overtime to support her?

I have already answered this question when I dealt with the breakdown of the marriage (see page 18). The rules which apply in divorce cases are similar – except that a divorced couple are no longer under a duty to maintain each other. The divorce court must consider your 'resources' and those of your wife, and supplementary benefit is not a resource. If you are in a position to make periodical payments to your former wife, the court will order you to do so. They will not allow you to throw on to the state the obligations which you yourself can and should bear; but they will acknowledge that in the vast majority of cases the split of one income between two families is bound to leave a hole which supplementary benefit will have to fill. Again, in many cases the only person who can claim benefit will be the wife – especially if she is at home looking after young children. A person cannot claim benefit if he or she is in full-time work. So in your case the court will make sure that your income does not fall below subsistence level; this may well mean that your wife will only get a modest order, and supplementary benefit will have to be called upon to make up the shortfall.

SUBSISTENCE LEVEL

What is subsistence level?

The courts have disagreed on this, but usually they take the supplementary benefit scales as their guide. A person's supplementary benefit comprises two basic elements:

1 normal requirements (a scale figure which changes in November every year); and

2 additional requirements in special cases (e.g. a special diet).

The courts will usually add these two items together and also your housing costs (as reduced by housing benefit). This will be your subsistence level, and the court will not allow your income to fall below it.

LONG-TERM SUPPLEMENTARY BENEFIT

I have been divorced for more than a year and, even with supplementary benefit, am finding it very hard to make ends meet. Can I go back to the DHSS and ask for more?

The answer may well be Yes. You will be entitled to an increase by going on to the 'long-term' scale. This can be claimed if

1 you have been receiving supplementary benefit for fifty-two weeks and
2 you have not been required to register for work throughout that time.

If, for example, you are a single parent looking after a child under 16, you will be able to satisfy this second condition. For the year starting in November 1982 the long-term rate for a single householder was £32.70 – an increase of £7 over the short-term rate.

PART-TIME WORK

That's useful, but it still isn't enough. Any other ideas?

Yes. If you can find a part-time job, there are two rules which may help you. Firstly, the first £4 can be disregarded – it won't cut down your supplementary benefit. Secondly, one-half of your part-time earnings between £4 and £20 is treated in the same way. So if you work one day a week and earn £18, you will be £11 better off than you were before, i.e.

$$\text{£}4 + \frac{18-4}{2} = \text{£}11$$

Only the balance of £7 will reduce your supplementary benefit.

LODGERS

What about taking in lodgers?

The rules here are even more favourable. If you do not spend 30 hours or more per week in looking after the lodgers, you can keep two-thirds of what you charge them without losing any part of your supplementary benefit. This is in addition to the other 'disregards' which I mentioned earlier. You must, of course, get the consent of the building society if you want to finance your mortgage in this way. Just one word of warning – don't cohabit with your lodgers because you may well lose all your supplementary benefit if you do (see page 159).

You said earlier that a court order for maintenance paid direct to a child could help to save tax. Would such an order also help my supplementary benefit position?

Not any more. The basic rule is that your resources and requirements must be added up with those of your dependent children. This means that any maintenance paid to the child over and above the scale figure for that child will be a 'resource' of yours and could cut down the amount of benefit to which you are entitled.

SUPPLEMENTARY BENEFIT AND CAPITAL

How does capital fit into all this?

The basic rule is that you can't get supplementary benefit if you have capital of more than £2,500. In arriving at this £2,500 figure the value of the home is not taken into account, and furniture will also be ignored. If, under the above rules, your total capital is £2,500 or less, then (apart from one special case) it won't cut down your supplementary benefit claim.

SUPPLEMENTARY BENEFIT AND LUMP SUMS

What is the special case?

There are very complicated rules about lump sums payable under an order made by the divorce court or magistrates' court. The effect of these rules (which only apply if they do not bring the total capital above £2,500) is to turn the lump sum into income; apparently the idea is that you should use the lump sum for living expenses for a set number of weeks. The number of weeks is found by applying the following formula:

$$\frac{\text{lump sum}}{\text{normal supplementary benefit claim} + 2}$$

So, let us suppose that the lump sum is £500 and that the wife normally receives supplementary benefit of £23 per week. The formula will be

$$\frac{500}{23 + 2} = 20$$

In other words the wife will be disqualified from supplementary benefits for 20 weeks!

Do these rules also apply where lump sums are paid to children?

Yes – but they only affect the benefit which can be claimed for those children and don't spill over into the parent's personal supplementary benefit entitlement.

I might add that the rules are even more complex where the order provides for periodical payments as well as a lump sum.

Are you saying that I shouldn't ask the court to give me a lump sum order?

A lump sum order could be very dangerous; you might spend the lump sum on house repairs or clothes, for example, and it will have run out before you can claim supplementary benefit again.

SINGLE PAYMENTS

But I urgently need some clothes for the children, the wallpaper is peeling off and they are threatening to cut off the gas. Where can I get the money?

It may be possible to ask the DHSS to let you have a single payment to meet an exceptional need. Unfortunately the rules are very tightly drawn. I think your best chance is in respect of the house repairs (for which the weekly 'housing cost' payment includes the princely sum of £1.50!). The rules allow you to claim a single payment for repair and redecoration if the total cost is £225 or less. On the question of clothing and heating you may have to fight on your hands because the DHSS will tell you that these items are covered by the normal weekly payment. Fortunately there is a 'safety-net' rule under which a payment must be made if the benefit officer is satisfied that payment is the only way of preventing serious damage or serious risk to the health or safety of yourself or your dependent children. The benefit officer must be satisfied that the needs cannot be met in any other way.

EMERGENCIES

I got fed up with sitting around at home and so I've just started a full-time job. On my second day I got a phone call from the police to say that my house had been damaged by fire; all the contents have been destroyed. Can I go back to supplementary benefit?

Yes. The rules allow payments to be made in urgent cases, and fire is given as an example. Payments can be made even where a person is not otherwise qualified to have supplementary benefit – for example, a person (like yourself) in a full-time job. Once again the rules are fairly tightly drawn, and in particular you may have to pay the money back.

What does the emergency relief cover?

It can cover living expenses, clothing, furniture, bedding, house repairs, fuel or travel and removal expenses. Again the rules are tightly drawn: you won't get a new table and chairs if secondhand ones are available, and you may even have to come to terms with a reconditioned cooker!

FAMILY INCOME SUPPLEMENT

I'm not getting much money from my husband and I want a full-time job. Unfortunately the wages in our area are very depressed and I'm only getting £40 per week. How can I get some more money?

If you have one or more dependent children you may be entitled to claim family income supplement if your total income (including maintenance and earnings, but *not* child benefit) is less than a specified amount. The current figure is £82.50 per week for a person with one dependent child, going up by £9 for each additional child.

How much will I get?

The benefit is worked out by applying this formula:

$$\frac{\text{Statutory figure} - \text{Your income}}{2}$$

So, if your total income is £50 per week and you have one dependent child you would get:

$$\frac{82.50 - 50}{2} = \text{£16.25 per week.}$$

I am expecting a rise in six months' time. Will my benefit be cut?

Strangely enough the answer is No. Once the amount of family income supplement has been worked out, it remains the same for 52 weeks.

If I do get supplementary benefit or family income supplement, will the DHSS put pressure on me to claim maintenance from my former husband?

No – it is not their policy to do this. Incidentally, I would like to remind you of a point which I made earlier (see page 17) – namely that, if you do get supplementary benefit (or indeed family income supplement), this will 'trigger off' certain additional benefits such as free prescriptions and sometimes free school meals. If the maintenance is too high, you may lose not only the main benefits but also these 'triggered benefits' too.

HOUSING BENEFITS

You have mentioned 'housing benefit'. What is this?

This is a benefit payable by local authorities under a new scheme coming into force in April 1983. If your income is below a certain amount you will qualify for 'housing benefit', giving you the right to a rebate on your rates (payable by the rating authority) and a rebate or allowance in respect of your rent (dealt with by the housing authority). These benefits are very valuable, and you must make sure you claim the full amount to which you are entitled.

I should add that the new scheme does not cover mortgage interest. This will still be dealt with by the DHSS as part of your supplementary benefit entitlement if you qualify for this.

BUYING A HOUSE ON SUPPLEMENTARY BENEFIT

Our house has got to be sold, and I'd like to buy another one; but I just don't see how I can afford it while I am on supplementary benefit. Any ideas?

First of all, a lump sum payment out of the proceeds of sale of your old house will not affect your right to supplementary benefit if it is earmarked for the new house. Secondly, the weekly payments of supplementary benefit should be sufficient to cover the mortgage interest. Thirdly, you may be able to pay at least part of the capital out of part-time earnings which will not necessarily cut into your supplementary benefit claim (see page 125). The building society may agree to such an arrangement if it is supported by a letter from the DHSS agreeing to pay the interest.

REMOVAL COSTS AND FURNITURE

Will the supplementary benefit help with the removal expenses, and will they also help me to furnish the house?

The answer to both questions may well be Yes. Removal expenses are payable if 'the move is due to . . . divorce or any other breakdown of marriage'. In such a case the DHSS will also provide furniture – although you may find it somewhat spartan! Once again the rules are tightly drawn and you should seek advice before you contact the DHSS.

6 Divorce and the Children

WHO GETS THEM

I have been a very good husband and father, but my wife has now left me and is living with another man. She has taken the children with her. I was very upset when you told me that my wife's conduct would not stop her getting maintenance. Now I suppose that you will add insult to injury by telling me that she will get the children as well. Is that right?

Ever since 1925 the courts have been under a duty to regard the welfare of the child as the first and paramount consideration. So they will have to look at all the circumstances in order to decide which of you is best able to promote the welfare of the child. In this sense I am afraid that your wife's conduct in leaving you is largely irrelevant – although her conduct (and yours) in relation to the children would be highly relevant.

In very many cases the mother does get custody of young children – especially if they are under the age of about ten. She will have spent a great deal of her time looking after them and in becoming familiar with their particular problems and will usually be in a better position than the father to offer 24-hour care. If you wanted to claim custody, you would have to satisfy the court that you could provide a normal family environment – including a 'mother substitute' who could look after the children (and cope with illness and emergencies) while you were out at work.

Another important point is that the courts are very reluctant to move the children around. You must, therefore, bring your custody claim just as soon as possible before the children are settled in their new home.

We have two children aged eight and six. If we get a divorce, they will stay with my wife, but I want to see them regularly and to have a say in their upbringing. What is the position?

There is an overwhelming need to come to an agreement with your wife about these matters and to do so at the earliest possible time. The supreme tragedy of divorce arises where bitterness over a failed marriage spills over into disputes over the children and where children are used as pawns in disputes over money. If you cannot agree, I would strongly urge you to get in touch with a conciliation service.. After all, the divorce may be over in a matter of months, but the relationship with your children lasts for a lifetime, and it is vitally important to get it right during the very sensitive adjustment period which follows separation or divorce. If you and your wife are sensible parents and are willing to cooperate with each other, you should agree on an order for joint custody with care and control to your wife. In this way your wife will be responsible for the day to day problems involved in bringing up the children, but the major decisions such as education will be decided by the two of you jointly.

All this is subject to the overriding factor which I have already mentioned: any court will always treat the welfare of the children as the first and paramount consideration. They are not bound to give effect to an agreement which you have reached with your wife; in practice, however, if you both show an attitude of total cooperation, the court is likely to make an order on the lines of your agreement.

If you can't come to an agreement along the lines I have suggested, the court is unlikely to make a joint custody order. In this situation the court is more likely to award custody to your wife with reasonable access to you. By getting an order for custody your wife will have the right and the duty to take the major decisions, and it seems (although the legal position is not entirely clear) that she does not have to consult you about them.

Can the divorce court grant custody to someone other than the husband or wife?

Yes. The divorce court can grant custody to anyone, but obviously the welfare of the child will be most carefully considered before any custody order is made.

Can custody be ordered even if the child is sixteen?

In theory it can be ordered at any time until the child attains eighteen, but it will not normally be ordered or enforced against the child's wishes once the child has attained sixteen. In exceptional cases, however, perhaps if the child is mentally retarded, an order can be made.

JEHOVAH'S WITNESSES

I am a very active member of the Jehovah's Witness sect, and my friends tell me that I will never get the custody of my son. Is that right?

No. The mere fact that you belong to that sect is irrelevant; what matters is how far, if at all, your behaviour towards your son will be harmful to his welfare. In one case, for example, a Jehovah's Witness parent was refused access to his son because the court was satisfied that he would use the access period to indoctrinate the child, thereby causing great emotional tension between the parents which was bound to cause harm to the child. On the other hand, the courts are fully prepared to grant custody or access to a Jehovah's Witness parent providing they are satisfied that

1 the child will receive normal medical care (including blood transfusions if necessary),
2 the child will not be excluded from ordinary life and

3 the child will not be encouraged to reject the other parent and his or her beliefs.

A welfare officer is likely to talk to you on these points before making a recommendation to the court.

BROTHERS AND SISTERS

My husband has suggested that he should have the boy, while I should have the girl. I'm not very happy with that arrangement. What would a court do?

The court is likely to decide that the welfare of the children is best served by keeping brothers and sisters together. It will therefore have to decide whether both children should stay with you or with their father.

WISHES OF THE CHILD

My son keeps on telling me that he wants to come and live with me. Will his views be considered by the court? Will the judge talk to him?

If your son is very young (perhaps seven or less) then the courts will not give a great deal of weight to his views. In other cases they will consider his views very seriously as one of the relevant factors. There are, however, two factors which must be borne in mind, namely

1 your son will not be the best judge of where his long-term interest lies and

2 he may have been coached.

Turning to your second question this is a very personal matter for the judge. Some judges do talk to the child – especially in cases where the other factors are evenly balanced. Other judges are less willing to interview the child and they have a legal right to refuse to do so.

THE NEW HUSBAND

My former wife is getting married again, and I don't think much of her fiancé. I'm sure he will be a bad influence on the children. Is this relevant?

Most certainly. In one case a wife became obsessed with a man whom the judge described as evil, bad, obnoxious, without principles and a philanderer. In another case the wife married a man with a number of criminal convictions (including one for unlawful wounding). In both cases the potential harm to the child led to the mother losing her claim for custody. You will obviously have to put forward a strong case showing why the fiancé would be a bad influence.

OPERATIONS

My husband has left me, but I haven't been to court yet. Our daughter needs an operation. Can I tell the hospital to go ahead, or do I have to tell my husband first and get his consent?

You and your husband share the parental rights and duties, and each of you can exercise them on your own without having to consult. Obviously it is desirable to let your husband know, but it is not legally essential.

EDUCATION

My wife has been given custody of our two girls after our divorce. I am a teacher, and my wife knows nothing about education. I am sure that she will send the children to the wrong school. What can I do about it?

Try to talk to her so that you can come to some agreement. If that doesn't work, you can go back to the court that made the order and ask the court to deal with it.

KIDNAPPING

We lived in America and got a divorce in California. I went on living there with the children, and the judge gave me custody. My husband has arranged for the children to be kidnapped and brought over to England, and I've found out the address where they are staying. What can I do to get them back?

You could just go along and take the children (if it is physically possible) or you could ask the court to return the children to you. In either case your former husband may respond by making the children 'wards of court'. This can be done very quickly and brings the children under the court's control. This means that you can't do anything to the children (such as taking them abroad) without the court's permission.

But he's kidnapped them. Surely I'll get them back?

You should get them back if you act quickly, but there is no absolute guarantee. I have said before that the welfare of the children is the first and paramount consideration, and this rule applies even in kidnapping cases. In one recent case the court granted care and control to a mother who had kidnapped the children in Israel and brought them to this country. A report prepared by a court welfare officer showed that the children had a happy and secure home with their mother, and the court had doubts about the fitness of the father to bring them up and about the welfare of the children in unfamiliar surroundings. Obviously the kidnapping is a relevant factor in all those cases, but it is not the only factor, and you must be prepared to deal with the general question of the children's upbringing if the matter comes to court.

EMIGRATION

I was born in Spain and lived there until I was twenty. I

married my husband in England, but it didn't work out, and we got divorced. The judge allowed me to keep our little girl. I have no friends over here, and I want to go back to my family in Spain and to bring up my child there. Can I do that?

The divorce court which gives custody to a parent always makes it a condition that the child shall not be taken out of England and Wales. This condition can cause hardship, and so the court tells you that you *can* take your child abroad if
1 you sign a form that you promise to return the child if the court asks you to do so and
2 your husband consents – unless the court decides that his consent is not necessary.

Now in your case the facts are rather special: you want to take the child out of England permanently. You must go back to the court to ask for the court's permission. Once again the welfare of the child is paramount, and a number of questions must be answered. How old is your daughter? Is she happily settled here? Is she at school? Will she be harmed in having to adjust to a country unfamiliar to her? Does your husband want to bring her up over here, and can he provide a stable and secure home? All these factors must be considered, but if your husband is unable or unwilling to look after the child effectively, I think that your chances of success are good.

WELFARE REPORTS

I am sure that my home will be the best one for the children, but my wife says the same thing about her home. How will the court decide between us?

If the court wants more information on this sort of matter, it can order a welfare officer's report. The welfare officer in the High Court in London is a full-time official working for the court; in other parts of the country the welfare officer will be a probation officer. He will usually visit the parents in their homes and will also talk to other people who have been in contact with the children – schoolteachers, doctors, health visitors and, in appropriate cases, other social workers. When he has done this he will prepare his report and will usually recommend who should look after the children. His report will be filed at court and will be a very important feature of the case.

Can we see his report?

Yes – the Registrar will tell you that you can inspect the report and order copies on payment of a fee.

Is the judge bound to do what the welfare officer recommends?

No, but he will attach a lot of weight to the report and, if he goes against the recommendation, should explain why he has decided to do so.

ACCESS

My former wife and I are on very bad terms, and she says that she won't let me see the children. Can she do that?

In the vast majority of cases the answer is No. The welfare of the child is usually served by allowing it to have regular contact with both its parents, and in most cases the parent who does not live with the children is granted reasonable access to them. The only case where access would be refused is where the court is satisfied that it would be harmful to the children. If, for example, they are normal and healthy children who become ill or violent or disturbed whenever their father comes to see them, then access will be refused. The mere fact that you and your wife are on very bad terms is not a ground for refusing access, although in bad cases arrangements may well be made that you should meet your children on ‘neutral ground’ (perhaps the home of a neighbour) so that you don’t have to meet your former wife.

I don’t mind them seeing their father but I don’t see why they should see that other woman. Will the court help me on this?

Almost certainly not. You are obviously very bitter about the failure of your marriage and are putting your emotions above the interests of the children. Access will usually be granted to a father because children have the right to keep in touch with both parents. Their welfare will usually be served if they see their father in a home environment (rather than just going with him to the park or to the pictures or to a football match.)

Will the court fix a timetable for access?

Only as a last resort. The timing of access should be a matter for agreement between the parents, and the order often provides for reasonable access. Unfortunately there are cases where a parent, recovering from the shock of a failed marriage, reacts by making difficulties over access. If agreement is not possible, the court will have to regulate it. A common order is that the children should go to stay with their father every other weekend, and the order will also deal with access during school holidays. The welfare officer may well be called in to make recommendations, but the judge will make the final decision. In the last resort the breach of an access order is punishable as contempt of court.

What should I do with the children when they do come to stay with me?

That is not a question for a lawyer. The ideal is to make the children feel that they have two homes to go to and two sets of parents to live with. It can be a sensitive matter at times; the one thing that you must never do is to rake over the past or do anything which will give the children a sense of insecurity.

I live in a one-roomed flat and so obviously can't have the children. My wife is often drunk and often leaves our eight-year-old twins alone at home. I think she is now in trouble with the police. What can the court do in a case like that?

Well, this could be one of those rare cases where the court would commit the children to the care of a local authority. This is very much a last resort and can only be used in exceptional cases. A survey of 652 cases showed that it was used in only two of them. Such an order would be varied if, for example, you got better housing, or if your wife turns over a new leaf and satisfies the court that she will be a responsible mother.

If my wife does say that she will look after the children properly, how can the court check up on this?

The court has another power which can be used in exceptional cases such as this. The court can place the children under the supervision of a local authority or welfare officer while they are in your wife's care. The order can deal with the matter in some detail – how often and where the supervisor can see the parents, his right to be told of a change of address and so on.

HOLDING UP THE DIVORCE

Do many judges hold up a divorce because of the children?

No. A survey of 95 divorces found that in only one of them was the judge not satisfied with the arrangements.

We are getting divorced, and I am unemployed. I can't look after the children because I am disabled. My wife, who goes out to work, does her best to look after the children with the help of neighbours, but sometimes it's difficult. What will happen on the divorce?

You cannot get a divorce unless the judge has made an order that the arrangements for the children are satisfactory, or the best that can be worked out in the circumstances, or that it is not practicable for the two parties to make such arrangements. I have already mentioned (see page 69) that, if you send in a divorce petition, you must also send in a 'statement of arrangements for children' dealing with your proposals – where will they live, where will they go to school, who is going to look after them financially and the arrangements for access.

Your wife can also put in her proposals. The registrar will arrange for the two of you to meet the judge in his room so that he can consider the arrangements. In this case I suppose the judge might suggest that the arrangement could be improved if your wife gave up work; whether he would do so would depend on whether this would mean a sharp drop in the family income. Alternatively it might be a case for involving the local authority (see above).

CHILD MAINTENANCE

My wife and I are getting divorced, and I want a 'clean break'. She can have the house and £10,000 for each child, but I don't want to have to pay any more under any circumstances. Can I make sure of this?

No. There cannot be a clean break where child maintenance is concerned. You have a duty to maintain your children, and the divorce court can make orders for their support from time to time. In one recent case a husband made a clean-break divorce settlement. Subsequently his wife had to draw supplementary benefit, and the DHSS successfully sued the former husband to recover sums paid for the children.

What financial orders can the court make for the children?

The orders are very similar to those I have described (see page 81), although it is fairly unusual to order a transfer of capital in favour of the children unless it is needed for some special purpose. The court can order

1 periodical payments,
2 a secured provision,
3 a lump sum or sums,
4 a transfer of property,
5 a settlement and
6 a variation of settlement.

The first four of these are subject to age limits and do not come to an end on the remarriage of the husband or wife.

What are the age limits?

Basically, an order for periodical payments can continue until the child is seventeen, but the court has wide powers to let it carry on until eighteen. It can also go on beyond this age if the child is still in education or training – or would be if the payments were made.

Can a child over eighteen get a lump sum order?

Only in the case I have just mentioned – if he or she is undergoing education or training.

I urgently need some money for the children, and there may be some delay before the divorce finally comes through. Can I get money before the divorce?

Yes, the court can make orders for child support before, on or at any time after the decree – and even if the divorce petition is dismissed altogether (perhaps because you have already been divorced abroad). How soon you can get some money will depend to a large extent on how quickly you can get a hearing date from the court. There will also have to be enough time for affidavits to be sworn and filed.

I have just had an angry letter from my daughter who is eighteen. She says that unless I pay her some money she is going to take me to court. The divorce took place two years ago, and my former wife and I have both remarried. Can my daughter really take me to court?

Yes. Although the divorce is over the court can make a child-support order not only when it grants the divorce but 'at any time thereafter'. In a 1976 case the court allowed a girl who was over eighteen to join in her parents' divorce and claim maintenance – even though the divorce had taken place some ten years previously!

Is there any top age limit at all in a case like this?

No. If your son or daughter is a student who keeps failing his or her examinations, your duty to maintain them can continue indefinitely while they are engaged in education or training.

We were a very happy family until we split up, and I paid £20 per week for her and the baby. She now tells me that the child wasn't mine, but that I've still got to go on supporting it because the father has disappeared. Can I be made to support the child? How much will I have to pay?

The answer to your first question is Yes. Both the divorce court and the magistrates' court can order you to support a 'child of the family', and these words include any child who was treated by your wife and yourself as a child of your family. In this case the law will assume that it is your child, and it will be up to you to prove (if you can) that the child is not yours. On the basic question, however, the position is clear: you have both treated the child as a child of your family, and therefore you are liable to support it.

On your second question there is no fixed amount, and the court must consider a number of points. They include the needs of the child, the family's standard of living before the breakdown and any disability from which the child is suffering. In the case of a child which is not yours the court must also consider

1 to what extent you supported the child financially,
2 whether you knew that the child was not yours and
3 the liability of any other person to maintain the child.

You should therefore tell the court what happened and argue very strongly that the child should be supported by its father (and/or the state) and not by yourself. Personally I think that many registrars would order you to pay something for the child, but the case could go either way.

BLOOD TESTS

We split up about a year ago and are now getting divorced. My wife has recently given birth to a child. She is claiming that I am liable to maintain it, but I don't think the child is mine. What can I do? Can the court order blood tests, and will they help me?

A child born to a married woman during her marriage is presumed to be the child of the husband, and so in your case it will be up to you to prove that the child is not yours. If you were having intercourse with your wife at the time when you left her, then clearly, from a biological point of view, the child *could* be yours. On the other hand, if you and your wife had not had intercourse for, say, eighteen months before the child was born, the court (if it believes your evidence) will inevitably decide that the child cannot be yours.

If you are in a 'borderline' situation, the court does have power to give directions for blood tests to be taken on yourself and on your wife. They cannot make an *order* for a blood test – in other words, a husband or wife will not be in contempt of court if he or she refuses a blood test – but the court will no doubt draw its own conclusions from such a refusal. The court also has power to order a blood test on the child itself if it considers that it would be in the child's interests that this should be done. In the great majority of cases it is in the public interest (and in the child's long-term interests) that the truth should be discovered by the best available evidence; a refusal of a blood test would leave the child with a nagging doubt for the rest of its life.

Blood tests are becoming highly sophisticated and may show conclusively that you cannot be the father of the child. If this is so, you will not be liable to maintain the child because you have never treated it as a child of the family.

One final point: you could have a look at the Register of Births to see whether your wife has registered you as the father of the child. If she has not done so, your evidence of non-paternity will be greatly strengthened.

STEPCHILDREN

When my wife divorced her first husband she was given the custody of her five-year-old son. He and I have become very fond of each other. Will I still be able to see him if I divorce my wife.

Yes. It seems from what you say that you and your wife treated the boy as a child of your family. On a divorce the court can grant you access to the boy and will do so if they consider that such an arrangement would be for his benefit.

CHILDREN IN CARE

When we got divorced I had a nervous breakdown and had to put the children into care. I am now a lot better and want to have them back, but the local authority are being difficult. Can I get them back?

The basic answer is Yes. If a child is received into care under the Child Care Act 1980, the local authority cannot keep the child against its parents' wishes. There is, however, one possible snag; the local authority can sometimes pass a resolution under which they take over all the rights of a parent – including the right to keep the child in care.

That sounds terrible: in what circumstances can they do this?

The Child Care Act 1980 has a list of cases where this can be done. It includes cases where a parent has abandoned the child or is unfit to look after the child by reason of mental illness, permanent disability, child neglect or 'habits and modes of life'.

Can they do this to my children without letting me know?

No. Unless you have already agreed in writing, they must let you know in writing straightaway that they have passed the resolution and must also tell you that you have a right to object.

What do I do if I want to object?

You have to send them what the Child Care Act calls a 'counter-notice' within one month of getting their notice. If you do that, then the local authority will have to take the matter to court, and the court will have to decide whether the local authority can keep the children in care.

Does that mean that it will be splashed all over the local papers?

No. The proceedings will take place in a juvenile court, and there are very strict rules about newspaper reporting and about the persons who can be in court when the case is heard.

I put my son into care when I was ill. Can I just go along and collect him?

It depends. If he has been in care for six months, you have got to give the authority twenty-eight days notice that you want him back. They can then go into the case and might pass a 'parental rights' resolution in which case the matter may have to go to court (see above). If your son has not been in care for six months, you can collect him straightaway without having to give twenty-eight days notice.

I don't think the local authority are doing any good for my son. Can I go to court about it?

There are two things that you can do. Firstly, you could go to a juvenile court and ask that they should cancel the resolution and let the child come home to you. You will have to show that it is in the child's interests that such an order should be made – perhaps because your personal circumstances are now a lot better. Secondly, you could go along to the High Court to have your son made a ward of court. If this is done, the court will control the upbringing of your son. There is a clash here: on the one hand you have the court with its duty to look after children, while on the other hand you have the local authority with duties given to it by Parliament. On the whole the court will opt for non-interference: if the local authority is carrying out its duties (on such matters as access, choice of school, medical treatment and discipline) the court will not interfere. These are matters within the discretion of the local authority. If, on the other hand, the local authority is *not* carrying out its duties, then the court *will* interfere.

7 After the Divorce

VARIATION

When I divorced my husband the court ordered him to pay me £10 per week. At that time he didn't have much money, but he's a lot better off now and has just inherited £40,000. Can I get the order increased?

Yes. The divorce court has wide powers to vary an order for periodical payments either up or down. The court will take all the circumstances into account – including any change in the means of the parties. It would seem that your chances of getting an increase are good.

On the question of a lump sum order I would have to have some further information. In particular I would want to know what happened on the divorce. If you asked for a lump sum, and if your application was dismissed, I'm afraid you can't come back for another one. You might also be in difficulties if the court awarded you a small lump sum at the time of the divorce – you can't now get another one. On the other hand, it may be that you have never asked for a lump sum; in that case the court may now allow you to claim it. Alternatively, you may have claimed a lump sum, but done nothing about it. If that is so, you can now ask the court to deal with it.

The court will consider all the various matters I mentioned in Chapter 4 (see page 82). If the marriage had not broken down, you would have benefitted from the £40,000 in some way, and I think you have a good chance of getting an order – if it is still possible for you to claim it.

The divorce court ordered me to pay my former wife £40 per week, and at that time I could just about afford it because my new wife helped with the mortgage. She has now stopped working because she is expecting a baby. I just can't afford the maintenance any more. Can I get it reduced?

This is the reverse situation to the one discussed in the previous question. The court may very well reduce the order because the circumstances have changed since the order was made. There is, of course, no guarantee that you will get a reduction, but you should certainly apply for one. The court will consider not only the changes which have taken place since the order was made, but also the overall position of both parties when your claim for variation is heard.

I was ordered to pay my wife a sum of £10,000 by ten equal instalments. I have paid the first two, but I can't pay any more because I've been made redundant. Can the court cancel the rest of the instalments?

No. The *amount* of the lump sum cannot be changed but the court does have the power to reduce the instalments, and in your case they may well do so.

I have just come out of hospital after an accident and the maintenance payments I was making to my former wife have fallen into arrears. From now on I can only do part-time work. Can I ask the court to cancel the arrears?

Yes. If your former wife brings proceedings to enforce the arrears, the court can 'remit' the arrears in whole or in part – in other words the arrears can be wiped out. Alternatively you could go to court for a reduction in the payments, and this reduction could be backdated to the date of your injury. This could have the indirect effect of wiping out the arrears in whole or in part.

When we got divorced last year, we had had a long fight about money. Eventually I was offered £2,000 in full and final settlement, and my solicitor told me that, on the basis of my husband's affidavit, I should take it. I now find that he's got a farm and two houses which he never told me about. Can I go back to the court to ask for some more money?

Yes. The court will probably have made a 'clean break' order (see page 88), but it seems that your husband didn't really come clean when it came to disclosing his assets. Your solicitor may well be able to get the court to set aside the order. When that has been done the court can take a fresh look at the case and give you more money if this would be the right thing to do. The whole question of your needs, your means and those of your ex-husband and all the other factors would have to be taken into account.

Could I get one of the houses?

I don't see why not. You will almost certainly have asked for a 'transfer of property' order in your divorce petition, and this means that the court will be able to deal with it when it cancels the 'full and final settlement' order.

But I never filed a divorce petition. I let my husband divorce me.

Don't worry. There are ways in which the court can allow you to ask for a transfer of property order, and then an order can be made.

My ex-wife has remarried, and I have only just found out. Can I get back the money which I have paid to her?

Not automatically. A maintenance order automatically comes to an end on the remarriage of the person receiving payments (the payee), but there is no automatic right to recover payments made in ignorance of the remarriage. Instead the court has a discretion to order repayment in whole or in part. If, for example, all the money has been spent, there is no guarantee that the court will order your former wife to pay the money back.

ENFORCEMENT

My ex-husband is always getting into arrears with his maintenance, and I just haven't bothered to chase him up. Is there any time limit for claiming arrears?

Yes. If the arrears are more than twelve months old, you must get the leave of the court before you can take steps to recover them, and the court may, if it thinks fit, cancel the arrears in whole or in part. If your former husband can show that he is ready, able and willing to pay the current maintenance if the burden of the arrears were lifted from his shoulders, then an order for cancellation of the arrears is quite likely.

My former husband enjoys a very high standard of living, but he never pays my maintenance on time. He is now several months in arrears and makes one excuse after another. Can he be sent to prison?

Yes. Imprisonment for most kinds of debt was abolished in 1970, but an exception was made for sums due under maintenance orders. In these cases a summons can be issued under the Debtors Act 1869, and your husband will have to attend the court to be questioned about his means. If the court is satisfied that he has failed to make the payments at a a time when he had the means to do so, the court can commit him to prison for up to six weeks. In practice a suspended order is sometimes made, and the threat of imprisonment may encourage your husband to find the money.

Will the imprisonment wipe out the arrears?

No, but your former husband cannot be imprisoned more than once for the same arrears.

What are the other ways of getting the money? What about writing to his bank, or to his firm or sending in the bailiffs?

All these can be useful in the right kind of case – although they can be frustrating, time-consuming and expensive. Let me look first at the bank. If there is a credit balance on your former husband's account, you can go to court (under a special procedure called 'garnishee') for an order that a sum equal to the arrears or the credit balance (whichever is the less) shall be paid by the bank direct to you and not to your former husband. The practical result of this is to freeze the whole or part of his bank account – and this itself may make him see the light! The court is not bound to make such an order. If, for example, your former husband cannot pay his debts, the court will not make an order which will give you an unfair advantage over the other creditors. For obvious reasons it is vital to move quickly and get a freezing order (even on a temporary basis) before your former husband finds out what is happening and draws all his money out.

As far as his employer is concerned it is possible to apply to the court for what is known as an 'attachment of earnings order'. This is an order which tells the employer to deduct a sum from your former husband's pay and to pay it to the court collecting officer. It sounds fine in theory, and perhaps your former husband might not be very keen for his firm to find out about his marital problems. In practice, however, it doesn't work very effectively. It doesn't cover self-employed people and your husband can frustrate the order just by changing his job (although the court must be notified of this by him and by any new employer who knows of the order).

A visit from the bailiff might also be unwelcome for your former husband, but you would have to consider whether any furniture, etc., sold by the bailiff would produce any surplus after paying the costs of the sale.

Is there some way of cutting down on all the expense of trying to get the money?

Well, if we are dealing with an order for periodical payments, you could apply to register the order in the magistrates' court. If the court makes an order for registration, the weekly or monthly payments will be made by your former husband direct to the court, and the clerk of the court will have the job of enforcing the order if it is not paid. Also, if you are receiving supplementary benefit, an order which is registered in the magistrates' court can be 'signed over' to the DHSS, as I have already explained on page 18.

The divorce court ordered my husband to transfer the house to me, but he has now disappeared and hasn't signed the deeds. What can I do?

Don't worry. The court can order someone else (e.g. a court registrar) to sign the deeds if your former husband fails to do so. You can issue a special summons to the court asking for this to be done.

BANKRUPTCY

Can I make him bankrupt?

If the default relates to maintenance arrears, then the answer is No; maintenance is not a fixed debt like other debts because of the wide powers of the court to vary the amount of maintenance and to wipe out arrears. On the other hand you could make him bankrupt if he was ordered to pay you a lump sum and didn't do so. Whether it will do you much good is another matter, but perhaps the threat of bankruptcy will, like the threat of imprisonment, have some effect.

REMARRIAGE

My ex-husband is paying maintenance under a court order for myself and the two children. I now want to remarry. Is there any way in which I can keep the order alive in case my new marriage doesn't work out?

No. The order in your favour will automatically end on your remarriage. The order in favour of the children will continue. I suppose your former husband might ask the court for a reduction on the basis that your new husband should contribute to their support, but I don't think he would be successful.

I divorced my husband last year and was given the custody of our son. I now want to get married again and to change the boy's surname to that of my new husband. Can I do so?

Not automatically. The court order giving you custody will almost certainly have contained a clause forbidding you to change the boy's name without the written consent of your former husband or the leave of the court. If your former husband does not agree to the change of name, you would be in contempt of court if you changed the child's name without a court order. The court has a complete discretion in the matter, and all relevant factors (long term and short term) will be taken into account in deciding where the child's interests lie. Some judges have regarded the name as relatively unimportant and have readily allowed a change; other judges (perhaps the majority) have regarded a change of name as a serious matter which could harm the child's interests by weakening his links with his father.

When we got divorced I was given the custody of our two daughters. Their father hasn't shown much interest in them. I got married again last year, and we are a very happy family. My new husband has now suggested that we should jointly adopt the girls so that he can become their legal father. Can we do this?

It is certainly possible, but it's not always very easy. The legal effect of the adoption would be to make the children for all purposes the children of the new family. The father of the children must consent to the adoption; if he does not consent, the adoption cannot go ahead unless the court decides that he is withholding consent unreasonably. Also, the adoption cannot go ahead if the court thinks that an order for custody or access made by the divorce court would be better for the children. In other words, a very difficult balancing decision must be made by the court. Will adoption be the best course for the children, or would it be better for them to remain legally the children of the natural parents? As the father does not show much interest in the children, the adoption may well be allowed to go ahead.

My wife divorced me last year and got married again as soon as the divorce came through. Her new husband has just been killed in a car crash, and she now wants me to pay her £10 per week as maintenance and to give her a share of the house. Do I have to pay her anything?

As regards maintenance the answer is No: any right to an order for payments automatically comes to an end on remarriage. With regard to the house we must find out whether she made a claim for it in her divorce petition (the chances are she did). If that is so, the claim can go ahead even after a remarriage although the remarriage is obviously a very relevant factor in deciding what order (if any) should be made. She might also have a claim if she made a substantial contribution to the purchase or improvement of the house.

My husband gave me the house when we got divorced, and I've just had a terrible shock. Apparently he has gone bankrupt, and his trustee in bankruptcy wants to turn me out and sell the house. Can't I just tell the trustee that the house is mine?

I'm afraid it's not as easy as that. The law has to strike a balance between the rights of creditors and the rights of the family. If the transfer was a voluntary one (in the sense that you didn't give anything up in return for the house), the trustee may be able to have the transfer to you upset at any time within ten years of the transfer. If, on the other hand, you gave up your right to maintenance, or agreed to accept reduced maintenance, then you may be able to keep the house after all. It could also be important to know whether you paid for the house in any way (perhaps the deposit, or the mortgage instalments) because this could also be a useful weapon against the trustee. It is a difficult area, and you must go to see a solicitor straightaway.

COHABITATION

We have now been divorced for two years, and I have become friendly with a colleague at work. He has asked me to move into his flat, but I am rather nervous of doing so. How will my financial position be affected?

If your ex-husband has been ordered to pay you maintenance, the order will not automatically come to an end if you start to live with another man. It is merely one factor which could be taken into account if your ex-husband applied for a variation of the order. If your new boyfriend pays for your food, clothing and household expenses, then clearly your financial needs are considerably reduced, and your ex-husband would be in a strong position to argue for a reduction in the order.

There may also be a problem if you have been drawing supplementary benefits. At present the law says that where a married couple or an unmarried couple are living together, the resources of the man and woman must be added together and only the man can claim. The key phrase 'living together as husband and wife' is not defined in the Supplementary Benefits Act, and the official supplementary benefit handbook gives us a list of six main criteria:

1 members of the same household,
2 stability,
3 financial support,
4 sexual relationship,
5 children and
6 public acknowledgement.

This does not mean that all of these factors must be present together; indeed the 'living together' test may be satisfied even though there is no financial support and even though no sexual intercourse takes place.

This all seems very unfair.

I think that the aggregation rule is fair enough; after all, why should an unmarried couple be better off financially than a married couple? I do agree with you that the rule whereby only the man can claim is unfair and, under pressure from the EEC, the law is going to be changed.

Would I lose my benefit as soon as I moved in to his flat? It might not work out.

Let me quote from the official supplementary benefit handbook. In the section dealing with the stability of the relationship it says this:
'Living together as husband and wife implies more than an occasional or very brief association. When a couple first live together, it may be clear from the start that the relationship is similar to that of husband and wife, e.g. the woman has taken the man's name and has borne his child; but in cases where the nature of the relationship is less clear the woman may continue to receive benefit for a short time in order to avoid discouraging the formation of a stable relationship.'

Would the position be different if I stayed in my flat, and we just spent our spare time together?

Yes. As regards the maintenance order the court is very unlikely to alter it unless there is a change in your financial position; the mere fact that you have a boyfriend is irrelevant. As regards supplementary benefit it is very unlikely that you will lose benefit because you can show that you and your boyfriend are keeping up two households; his sometimes spending the night at your flat is in no way a reason for depriving you of your benefit. If they try to cut off your benefit, you should appeal, and your chances of success are good.

Two years ago I got divorced and three months ago I got engaged to be married again. I paid £1,000 for a caterer and £2,000 for the furnishing of a flat where we were going to live. Yesterday I had a note from my fiancé to say that he's changed his mind. To add insult to injury he has asked for his ring back. What is my legal position?

First, the good news – you can keep the ring. In theory, a man can say to his fiancée, 'I am putting this ring on your finger on the clear understanding that it must be returned to me if the marriage does not take place' (or words to that effect), but I am sure that any such engagement would be very short! In the normal case an engagement ring is an outright gift to the girl.

Now for the bad news. The old action for breach of promise of marriage (which you may remember from *Trial by Jury*) was abolished in 1970. The result is that you have no legal claim against your fiancé for the wasted expenditure.

My husband divorced me last year, and we have both re-married. My new husband has asked me why I never claimed a share of the house. I suppose I never thought I might have a claim. Is it too late to make a claim now?

No. It is too late to ask the divorce court to give you a share in the house because of your contribution to the welfare of the family (your work in the home, bringing up the children and so on). You may still, however, be able to show that part of the house belongs to you because you made a substantial money contribution to the purchase or improvement of the house.

The mortgage was paid by standing order out of our joint account. Will that help?

Yes – if you both paid money into the account so that it was a 'joint purse'. In that sort of case the principle of 'joint ownership' may well cover not only the bank account itself, but also property paid for out of the account. There is, of course, no guarantee that you will get a half share: a lot will depend on how much you put in. If, for example, you only paid money in for one year (before your first child was born), while your husband has paid in for ten years, then the proportion you will get could be quite small.

I took in lodgers – would that help?

Yes, I think it would. You must try to show some arrangement under which you agreed to pay some of the bills from your earnings so that your husband could use his income to pay the mortgage.

PENSIONS

I haven't worked for twenty years, but after divorcing my husband I have started again. Will I get a state retirement pension when I am 60?

The rules are very complex, but the answer may well be Yes.

Your rights will depend on your contribution record during your 'working life', and this will be from 16 to 59. Obviously, you are now paying contributions, but there seems to be a nasty 20-year gap in your contribution record. However, there are two special rules which will help you. First of all, you will be able to take advantage of what is called 'home responsibilities protection'. This allows you to disregard any years throughout which (for example) you were receiving child benefit for a child under 16. Secondly, you can rely on contributions paid by your former husband from the start of your working life until the year of your divorce. When you take these two rules and add on the contributions which you are paying now, the position may not be quite so bad after all.

Anything else?

Yes. You will only get the pension if you retire – although this rule won't stop you claiming it when you reach 65. The position will also be very different if you are a member of a private pension scheme which is contracted out of the state scheme. If you belong to a scheme, then you should have a booklet which explains this to you.

I've been lonely since I divorced my husband and am thinking of getting married again. Will this affect my pension rights?

Yes. First of all, your new husband may well belong to a company pension scheme. Such schemes will usually provide benefits for a widow, and you will be his widow (if you are still married to him when he dies). Secondly, if your new husband dies before retirement his pension scheme will usually give a large tax-free lump sum (perhaps four times his final salary) to a person chosen by him. I am not suggesting that you make it a condition of marriage that he makes you the beneficiary, but you might just mention it to him at a suitable time! Thirdly, you can rely on his contributions to qualify you for your own state retirement pension. Fourthly, if you are married to him when he dies, you will be entitled to certain state benefits (widow's allowance, widow's pension, widowed mother's allowance) based on your new husband's contribution record.

What about the contributions my ex-husband paid?

You can't have your cake and eat it! If you remarry, you will have the benefit of your new husband's contributions, but you will lose the benefit of your ex-husband's – unless you can postpone the wedding until you are sixty!

I've made a will leaving everything to the children. Will I have to change it if I get married again?

You have no choice. A will is automatically revoked by marriage so that your existing will can be thrown away as soon as you remarry. The idea behind this rule is that you will probably want to change your will anyway so that you can give some of your property to your new partner and/or to any future children that you may have.

But I don't want to change it.

That doesn't alter the basic rule that the will has no legal effect once you have got married.

So what should I do?

After the marriage you can make a new will leaving your property in the same way as before. You could also ask your solicitor to draw up a short document which will 'revive' the old will – i.e., bring it back to life.

Can I write my new will before I get married?

Yes, but you must use a special form of wording. You should refer in your will to your forthcoming marriage by using words such as: 'I make this will in contemplation of my marriage to Jane Smith.' This should stop the will being revoked when you do marry Jane Smith.

I've just realised that in my will I have left a lot of money to my ex-wife. Will she still get it even though we are divorced?

A very recent Act of Parliament has changed the law. Where a gift to a spouse is followed by a divorce the gift is, in effect, cancelled out. If this new rule applies in your case, the answer to your question is No. The exact position will depend on the date of the divorce, and you should get advice on this point from a solicitor.

My former husband has just died owning a large house and a very successful chain of shops. I worked in the business for many years before the divorce, and my new husband tells me that I should claim that half of the house and business is mine. Is he right?

First of all, any claim you may have has not been lost by your remarriage. We are not dealing here with the power of the divorce court to alter property rights: your claim would be made on the basis that part of the house and part of the business are yours because of your work.

Let me first deal with the business. If it was a joint business run by your ex-husband and yourself, I think that you have a very strong claim – but I don't think you would get half. The court would probably give you a share based on the value of the assets (including goodwill) when you left the business. If you merely worked in your husband's business, then your claim is not so strong: you would have to show that you worked there without pay or at an uneconomic wage, so that the business could be built up for the benefit of both of you.

On the question of the house, if the deeds are in your joint names, you may well be entitled to half of it. You may even be entitled to the *whole* of it – although this would depend on the actual wording of the deeds. In some cases property which is owned jointly (whether by a married couple or by other people) passes automatically to the survivor.

If the house is in your ex-husband's name, you can still have a claim if for example

1 you paid the deposit or
2 you paid off a large part of the mortgage or
3 you paid money for improvements or
4 you worked without pay or at an uneconomic wage in the business so that your then husband could use the profits to pay for the house.

Whether you would get a half share, or more or less, would depend on how much you and he each put in.

Presumably there will be a lot of capital transfer tax to pay on the death?

Tax is only payable on property owned by your ex-husband (and no tax is payable on one-half of the value of business assets). The rules which I have just explained will not only give you a right to claim a share of the assets, but they will also reduce the tax bill, because that share has never belonged to your ex-husband, and therefore it is not taxable as part of his estate.

My former husband has just died. Presumably I can't claim widow's benefit because we have been divorced. Can I claim anything else?

Yes. You may be entitled to a benefit called 'child special allowance'. This benefit is available if

1 you are looking after one or more children and
2 your late ex-husband was maintaining them and
3 he has paid or been credited with sufficient contributions.

Can you tell me something more about this benefit?

The benefit is payable at a flat rate for each child living with or supported by you if the child is under 16, or under 19 and engaged in full-time education. In the year commencing 23rd November 1982 the rate was £7.95 per week. It is payable in addition to child benefit and is tax free. It is not payable if you have remarried and is suspended while you are living with another man as his wife.

We were divorced three years ago, and the court ordered my former husband to pay me £2,000 a year and to allow me to go on living in the house for the rest of my life. I've had a letter from his solicitor to say that my former husband has just died and that his will leaves nothing to me. What are my legal rights?

First of all, the maintenance order has now come to an end, and you can't claim any more money under the order (except for money owing when he died). Your right to go on living in the house is probably unaffected by the death – although you must look closely at the exact wording of the order. Finally, you could bring a claim under the Inheritance (Provision for Family and Dependants) Act 1975 for an order on the ground that he has failed to make reasonable provision for you after his death. Whether you will succeed in getting an order is a difficult question which will depend on your resources, the size of the estate and the obligations of your late husband to his children, to any new wife and to other persons. If, for example, your former husband had substantial capital assets, or if money becomes payable to the estate under an insurance policy or pension fund, then you might well get an order to compensate you for your lost income.

My wife and I lost contact after we split up. Last week I read in the paper that she had died. I wrote to her solicitor and was horrified when he told me that my wife had divorced me six months ago. How could that have happened, and can I do anything about it?

On page 70 I explained that, in certain cases, a divorce could be obtained against a missing spouse: the petitioner would tell the registrar that all possible enquiries had been made, and the registrar could then allow the case to go ahead even though the missing spouse would not know about it (he would 'dispense with service of the petition on the respondent'). I imagine that this has happened in your case.

If you want to do anything about it you should immediately see a solicitor who can find out more details about how the divorce was allowed to go through. There was a case in the courts in 1981 where the facts were very similar to those in your case. The court had a look at the divorce and found that the husband had not made enough enquiries when he got his order from the registrar. The court then cancelled the divorce – even though the husband had died.

Useful Addresses

There are a large number of agencies offering help, information and advice to persons with marital difficulties – whether or not a divorce is planned. They include the following:

National Marriage Guidance Council, Little Church Street, Rugby.

Local Marriage Guidance Councils. Addresses can be found in local telephone directories or from the National Marriage Guidance Council (above).

National Association of Citizens Advice Bureaux, 110 Drury Lane, London WC2.

Local Citizens Advice Bureaux (C.A.B.). The addresses can be found from the local telephone directory or from public libraries.

Probation and after-care services. The probation officers (whose work in connection with children is described in Chapter 6) have various local offices, and the addresses can be found from the local telephone directory. They have also recently started to run Divorce Experience courses in many parts of the country.

National Council for the Divorced and Separated, 13 High Street, Little Shelford, Cambridge, deal with postal enquiries from members of the public. The Council also operates counselling centres at Arborfield (Berks), Birmingham, Farnborough (Hants), Huddersfield, Isle of Wight, Lincoln, Norwich and Portsmouth. The addresses of these centres can be obtained from the Cambridge headquarters (see above) or from local Citizens Advice Bureaux.

Divorce Conciliation and Advisory Service, 38 Ebury Street, London SW1W 0LU. This is a private organization which offers help on divorce-related problems. A fee of £15 is payable for the initial consultation; subsequent fees are in the region of £10 per hour or less according to means.

Conciliation centres

Family Conciliation Bureau, Barnet, Divorce Court Welfare Services, 7c High Street, Barnet, Herts.

Bristol Courts Family Conciliation Service, 59 Broad Street, Bristol BS1 2EJ.

Bromley Family Conciliation Bureau, 5 Upper Park Road, Bromley, Kent.

Cleveland Family Conciliation Service, 34/36 Baker Street, Middlesborough, Cleveland TS1 2LH.

Coventry Family Conciliation Service, Fleet House, Corporation Street, Coventry.

(Dorking) Family Conciliation Service, 155 High Street, Dorking, Surrey.

Leeds Family Mediation Service, 36a Boar Lane, Leeds 1.

(Luton) Family Conciliation Service, The Court House, Stuart Place, Luton LU1 5DL.

Newton Conciliation Service, 20 Baxter Road, London E16.

Somerset Conciliation Service, 37 Chamberlain Street, Wells BA5 2PQ.

Sunderland Family Conciliation Service, 17 Hillside, Sunderland.

Swindon Family Conciliation Service, Courts of Justice, Princes Street, Swindon, Wilts.

Conciliation is very much a growth area, and a telephone call to the local probation service (see above) will reveal whether any new services have been set up in your area.

Index